Food for Thought

THE JOY OF LIVING
A Delicious & Nutritious Financial Life

ANITA SAULITE

Copyright © 2015 Anita Saulite

All rights reserved. No part of this publication may be reproduced, stored, in a retrieval system, or transmitted in any form or by any means, without prior written permission of the author.

Anita Saulite, MBA

www.anitasaulite.com
anita@anitasaulite.com
Twitter: @AnitaSaulite1
Facebook: Savvymoneygal

Library and Archives Canada Cataloguing in Publication

Book: 978-0-9940073-0-8
ebook: 978-0-9940073-1-5

Editing and proof reading: Sylvia Taylor

Book design, layout and typesetting: Vancouver Desktop Publishing Centre
Photo of Anita Saulite: Christopher Gentile Photography
Cover and inside photos: royalty free images from istock.com
Published in Toronto, Canada

Disclaimer: This book provides content for general information purposes and does not intend to replace professional advice. The content should not be relied upon for investing or financial services advice or the endorsement of others. Consult with professionals to understand the personal, investment, legal and tax implications to your own financial situation. The content of this book is based on information that is accurate and reliable at this time and is not guaranteed.

For my Mom — the best home cook and role model a woman could have!

AUTHOR'S NOTE

This book shares true stories and anecdotes of women I have met, coached or worked with in some capacity. There are limited identifying details in order to protect privacy under the Privacy Laws in Canada. Only I am identified using my real name, experts in their respective fields and their respective publications or research.

Limited information and primarily research presented in this book has been published before and may have appeared in *The Savvy Money Gal* or The Huffington Post Canada blog.

The 20th Century old stone farm house is a real home. The descriptions and surroundings of the old stone farm house are accurate with limited embellishment in order to augment the rural setting. Anita Saulite is a home cook, and from this perspective she shares her understanding and experience of the culinary world.

—Anita Saulite

DEDICATION

"Remember, No one's more important than people! In other words, friendship is the most important thing—not career or housework, or one's fatigue—and it needs to be tended and nurtured."

—JULIA CHILD

I dedicate this book to Hockey Moms across Canada: women I have met in small and large community centres in the wee hours of the morning, on weekends and late at night. We Moms sit together in the bleachers, cheering on our kids as they play hockey. Up there in our 'boardroom' we also share the vital details of our lives as mothers, wage-earners, entrepreneurs, partners and women trying to figure out how to thrive, find greater joy and live by our values. Those discussions gave me *Food For Thought* and helped me develop a menu for living a delicious and nutritious financial life. I am sending a heartfelt thank you to each and every one of you.

ACKNOWLEDGEMENTS

There are so many wonderful people whose support played a part in this book coming into being. I would like to thank the following associations, organizations, peers, friends and family for your support, encouragement and patience with me at every stage of this book.

TD Waterhouse, BMO Bank of Montreal, Retirement and Financial Planning, Private Client Group, RBC Dominion Securities, Scotiabank International and Retail Banking, and CIBC Business Banking Services, for allowing me to be part of your organizations at some point over the last twenty years and providing the solid framework and experience this book offers.

The Financial Planning Standards Council and The Investment Funds Institute of Canada (IFIC) in helping to shape and influence our investment and financial planning community. Your teachings around investing, the value of advice and the importance of financial planning are captured throughout this book working in orchestration with me to achieve the same outcomes.

The Canadian Women's Foundation for the excellent work they do in Canada helping women and children boost their wellbeing and for reaching out to me to be part of the leadership team in Vancouver and Toronto. I am humbled to work with you.

Nina Mazar for your best-in-class research on consumer behaviour, how financial literacy is only the beginning and how real change can only come through behaviour modification. And how knowledge and numeracy are essential and foundational and requires direction on how to optimize each into better financial outcomes.

Ian Whiting for your insight on investing behaviour and for publishing my articles every quarter in Money Magazine. Your thought leadership and approach to financial planning is making a difference in Canadians' livelihood.

The Huffington Post for giving me a national platform to write, share my insights, knowledge and thought leadership around personal finance wealth management. It has been a wonderful journey over the last year. I look forward to bringing more thought provoking and relevant content in year two.

Talbot Stevens for your advice and coaching on writing this, my second book. I appreciate your insider knowledge of what makes a good book, your willingness to share your experiences and a deep understanding of the financial services community.

Sylvia Taylor, my editor. Not only did we connect on a very personal level, but she understood my deep desire to write a book in my own voice. She appreciated the depth and breadth of my knowledge and helped me craft my message in a way that would be easy to read. Each time I reached the invisible wall, she gave me a gentle nudge to help me overcome barriers and road blocks. She felt my resistance, yet she let me problem solve, the thing I do best. Each time I showed up, she reminded me of the bigger picture. She knew I wouldn't be satisfied with publishing something that was half-baked, given my ability. Her impeccable skills in her craft became clear to me early in our work together and how everything we put on our tables, matters. Nothing is random. 'Breaking bread' and 'cooking' with Sylvia was a pleasure. We found the right balance between engineering, business and the 'kitchen.'

Patty Osborne for your detail to attention in design and layout. But most importantly for your patience around finding the best images for this book!

Craig Shemilt, for your guidance around production of my book, and how best to package it for my readers.

My dear friends in Vancouver and Toronto. I want to express my gratitude for welcoming me into your homes and community.
You were a constant reminder to me about the importance of life experiences and the value of relationships.

My family and my extended family. Everyday we prepare our meals together, gather at the table, sit side-by-side and enrich each other's lives. We always find a way to take the ordinary in our lives and make it extraordinary. Laughter is our constant companion and through storytelling we learn about each other and experience the joy of living.

Crave More

FIND INSPIRATION

Each of us needs to find inspiration in our lives. Inspiration can come from virtually anywhere. It's a driving force in helping us shape our lives and fulfill our wildest dreams and goals. I look for inspiration every day. I am inspired by the sound of the ocean, walking in a dense forest or just watching people live. I am inspired to live every day with greater intent and joy. I allow my mind to wander to places where I find clarity and vision.

When I started writing this book, I wanted to inspire women and offer something fun and exciting, beyond the ordinary, that would delight and refresh. I looked for inspiration in places where I find comfort. I found the perfect theme and setting for this book. Oddly enough, it came from something as simple as nibbling on a two-bite brownie®, a tiny but delicious morsel of chocolate, delectable enough to please the palate but small enough to assuage any guilty thoughts. It gave me food for thought on how simple life would be if all of us had a life and financial plan or our own 'two-bite brownie.' Its moneylicious, don't you think? I took it one step further. We find comfort and joy in our kitchen. The kitchen is at the heart of any home. We can bake or cook the simplest dishes but the time we spend together and our conversations is what really nourish us. Communication is at the heart of women. We share stories and laugh, and working in the kitchen becomes fun, inspiring and meaningful.

I began to research some of the leading culinary personalities in the world for inspiration. I was drawn to Julia Child. Much has been written about her and the movie "Julie & Julia" was a hit. This aside, what drew me to her was that her philosophy and approach to life was unquestionably authentic, real and refreshing. She had charm, wit and candor. Qualities I value and that resonate with me. What also inspired me was that Julia Child had many careers in her life. She didn't begin her culinary career until she was in her late thirties. She offered teachings for all of us. She lived by her values. She found humour in the smallest things and never took herself too seriously. She lived with intent and purpose. She found meaning in her work and joy in cooking. Her success came about organically through old fashioned hard work. She was an innovator in the kitchen. And finally, Julia Child lived to a ripe old age of ninety-two. She passed away in 2004. Her longevity no doubt came from living like the French, eating well and drinking fine red wine!

Most of us crave for more but sometimes figuring out what more is becomes the challenge. Julia Child searched for more. She never dreamed she would become famous or change North American cuisine by bringing French cuisine to the masses. She arrived in France with no purpose or direction in life. She made millions of dollars. Money or fame was not her intent or goal, rather, finding meaningful work that gave her joy. She saw money as a tool to help her cook, live and enjoy life. What better person to serve up to you as a role model?

All this gave me *Food For Thought.* Her life's journey inspired me to write this book. I promise you will experience the joy of living a delicious and nutritious financial life as we break bread together.

EVERYDAY SHOPPING

Before we go shopping for our groceries, most of us check our pantries or cupboards to see what we need to replenish, what's running low. In order to plan our daily and weekly meals we need to stock up on the right ingredients. We create our shopping list and head over to the grocery store with a plan. Our list keeps us focused so we are not enticed by impulse items at the end of the aisle or checkout that fill our grocery carts with things we really don't need. We have a focused strategy and plan, but alas, it's only grocery shopping.

Creating a Life Plan is not dissimilar to creating a list for our groceries. The first thing we need to do is take inventory of our lives and determine what we lack in order to help us figure out our goals. We may find it easier to figure out what we don't want based on past experience or knowledge. However, our goal is to stack our shelves and load up our pantries with what we want in life, have a clear sense of purpose and find joyful living every day.

Let's take stock of your life and where you are today. Take a few moments to nibble and chew on the following questions about you. We will refer to them later in this book but they serve a purpose now to get you thinking about your life as a pantry.

1. Where do you find yourself today? What's in your cupboards? What is lacking in your life? What gaps are you trying to fill?

_____

_____

2. Do you feel you have a purpose or intent in your life? If no, why not? If yes, please describe it.

_____

_____

3. What do you hunger for in your life? What would completely fill you up and bring you joy?

_____

_____

4. What is stopping you from filling up? What essential ingredients are you missing?

_____

_____

5. What nourishment, supplies and tools do you need? What do you need to learn about?

_____

_____

This will be the beginning for us. The intent in doing this mini-exercise early is to get you thinking about what gaps you may have in your life and to reflect on your life.

Here is an excellent example of an answer given by a young and very talented lawyer, completed for me at a "Women & Money" workshop in Vancouver, Canada.

"I am beginning to set up a family and build my career. Setting boundaries that will hopefully guide me. Building a secure and rewarding practise—always balanced with

my top priority being my family and health. I often have competing demands on my time. I will need the following in life to be successful: patience, discipline, structure, focus, balance, and being present."

Now that we know what we have, what we want and what we need, let's create a menu for you that is both delicious and nutritious.

❧ FEATURED MENU ☙

Welcome
Pull Up A Chair Around My Oak Harvest Table / 25

Starters and Appetizers
Tasty Tidbits: Success / 33

The Main Course
Relationships / 43
Everyday Living / 54
Health & Wellness / 73

A la Carte Menu
Create A Menu Just For You / 79

Dessert
Retirement / 93

Tools in the Kitchen
The Cast Iron Skillet: Money / 99
The Food Processor: Financial Planning / 119

Future Dinner Parties
Hungry For More / 135

Thanks For Joining Me Around the Table
Mi Casa es Su Casa / 159

Kitchen Utensils And Supplies
Essential Ingredients / 163

The Best Chefs in the World / 168
Not Your Average Home Cooks / 171

Welcome

PULL UP A CHAIR AROUND MY OAK HARVEST TABLE

"The main thing is to have a gutsy approach and use your head."

—JULIA CHILD

Thank you for joining me in my home: a quaint and charming 20th Century old stone farmhouse surrounded by evergreens, oak trees and shrubbery with a wonderful view of the lake. I am excited to have you here in my kitchen, around my old oak table, sipping coffee and nibbling on homemade cookies. Joining us will be Carol, Amanda, Susan, and June. Four dear friends that I think you will connect with instantly. It took me a long time to plan this event! I want our time together to nourish, fill and leave you content because I know our minds are hungry and need to be nourished too.

I am not a celebrity nor do I run a major corporation. I am a home cook, foodie, a wine connoisseur and lover of all things chocolate. I am also an executive, consultant, author, coach, wife, mom, friend, mentor and sister. Like you, I am many things to many people and have many different relationships.

Before I begin to share with you what you can expect on this wonderful culinary journey, I want to give you a quick peak into my life: where I have been, where I am today, and my plans for the future. Over the past twenty years I have worked in some capacity with all of the major banks in Canada. This experience was rich and rewarding. I learned first-hand what matters to people and the impact of money.

Over the years I have leveraged approaches used in business in all areas of my life. Mid-career I went back to school to pursue an Executive MBA at the Richard Ivey School of Business to quench my thirst for learning and to broaden my perspective of the world. Many of you would probably agree with me that the world of business teaches us the importance of strategic planning, innovation, flawless execution and managing profit and loss statements.

Companies have at their disposal, tools and resources to differentiate and find a compelling competitive advantage. They balance financial and human capital in order to find the right mix between corporate profits and employee satisfaction. They know that dissatisfied employees will not work hard while happy employees will be engaged and push through strategies in their everyday work resulting in the outcomes they seek. You don't have to have a career in the corporate world to understand the importance of strategy and planning while staying within a predefined budget.

While in business school in 2010, my MBA class was introduced to the Balanced Scorecard, a tool business uses to evaluate performance. The Balanced Scorecard is a technical approach rich in theory and application. It uses a combination of non-financial and financial measures to evaluate performance. For example, a non-financial measure could be customer experience or satisfaction where a financial measure could be net income, how much the company made in profits after expenses. The point is, companies use tools to measure performance.

Most of us would agree that companies are under enormous pressure to serve up shareholder returns in the double digits. They are in a pressure cooker of sorts to constantly achieve and exceed shareholder value or risk having their stock sold in favour of a substitute or company that can achieve better financial outcomes. As women, many of us feel the same pressure in our lives. We feel the pressure to take on more responsibilities at work and to make more money.

Some of us may evaluate our success by financial measures: how much money we earn, how much money we have invested or in our accounts, the market value of our homes, cars and other material items. But would this measurement be accurate as a metric to reflect success in our life? Isn't having a lot of money, toys and things irrelevant without friends and family to share the wealth or being healthy? Most of us would agree with this statement. If we take the lead from business and measure our lives using a series of financial and non-financial measures we may be able to find that right recipe and menu for living.

This is the thought leadership I bring to this book.

As a Financial Services Executive, Consultant and Coach, I help women get their money working for them that will pay for their dreams into their vibrant elder years. I demonstrate how money is a tool for living.

As a Certified Life Coach, I help women create a life strategy and plan that builds clarity and momentum. It offers the balance women seek and aligns to what they value.

Now, if you are starting to worry because you're not sure what a Life Plan is, I can assure you that you are not alone and we'll work together to cook up something wonderful. The number of women who've made this part of their life is small. And the number of women with a plan for their money is even smaller. Let's change that.

But when we find women who have a Life Plan and a Financial Plan… well, break out the French champagne! It's time to celebrate.

I also know about the things that stop women from achieving the success and joy they seek and deserve. Think of it like a missing spice that can pull everything together and have healing effects.

Over the past few years, I have travelled across Canada and had my feet on the streets in Toronto, Calgary and Vancouver. You shared your community, your homes and intimate stories about your life and how you feel about money. Some told me flat out that you are not looking for another book on personal finances or money management. The only way you would read one is if someone insisted, much like taking cod liver oil. A book on budgeting, saving, investing, credit card debt, planning and retirement? Please, no! A book on Life Planning strategies that addresses what matters to you, relationships, everyday living and health & wellness and connects to your money? Yes, please!

Please join me in this life menu stocked full of cooking and food metaphors. I invite you to explore possibilities that matter to you, as individual as you are. I want you to see yourself seated around my kitchen table, happy and relaxed with the other guests I have invited. Let's start.

As many of you may know, a well-designed home is built around the kitchen. The kitchen is the heart of the home. Martha Stewart believes that each kitchen has a personality and reflects the woman in it. This is the place where everything important happens, including eating delicious and nutritious food, trying new recipes and of course, spending time with loved ones.

My kitchen is mindfully laid out at the back of my home overlooking the lake. Nothing was random about its construction at all. It's stylish, rustic yet sophisticated, brimming with energy, focus and clarity. I share my home with my family and dog. Their presence fills every room.

Many of you will share your home with family, friends or guests. Today, the home has become a bigger community for many of us as our parents grow old with us. We care for the young. We care for the old. Our homes must welcome and invite those around us.

Some believe that the family health and fortune depends on the energy of the kitchen and the energy of the woman in the home. The design, its location and shape, can either create good or bad luck, including love and happiness. As in Feng Shui, my kitchen has all of the elements to create balanced wellbeing: fire, wood, water, metal and earth.

For millennia, the kitchen has been a place where women gathered to share stories of their lives, their family history and their deepest darkest secrets. Today, the walls in my home will speak of other women's stories and your story. Our mothers and grandmothers gathered in their kitchens to nourish us. They taught us the wonders of cooking and passed down family recipes, traditions, values and folklore. Sharing and passing down recipes to loved ones is a way we honour our mothers, grandmothers and other women who came before us. They are as important as love and shelter in our lives. We can learn from others' stories by sharing a part of us with them. Before we sit down, let's fill your cup to the brim and get to know each other better.

Food is a universal need. Mealtime brings us together to share, nurture and love one another. A diet full of rich, organic and nutritious food balanced across the major food groups supports the body to thrive. A Life Plan that captures our hearts and minds will offer intent, greater meaning in life and joy.

Meal planning is like Life Planning. You require a menu, good recipes to follow, the freshest ingredients, and the right tools in the kitchen. Ideas progress sequentially and they must be fully cooked to be of value. Heat develops ideas in the kitchen. Time allows a Life Plan to unfold. And with two essential tools in your kitchen, a cast iron skillet (money) and a food processor (financial planning) you will have everything you need to create a Life Plan and find the success you seek. Your plan will stand the test of time and you will want to share it with those near and dear to you. I promise you will leave satisfied. I designed this 'cook' book for you! Find the joy of living a nutritious and delicious (financial) life today.

The Table is Set for Guests

The excitement we feel when planning a dinner party is a combination of nerves and elation that something wonderful is about to unfold. The air in our home smells sweet. It is full of scents from our home cooking. Fresh flowers are mindfully placed in parts of our home. We want everything to look and be just right. Everything we put on our tables, matters. Everything we do in life, matters.

Whether it is lavish or simple, a well-dressed table is timeless and inviting. It starts with the basics. The tablecloth is the perfect size and just hangs over the sides of the table to skirt it but not interfere with guests at the table. We can also use a table runner to add colour and definition to the table. There is room for a centrepiece. A clear vase with freshly cut flowers adorns our table.

Each glass, dinner plate, soup and salad dish are set in front of each chair. The dishes can be either casual or formal. We could easily select our everyday dishes or fine bone china. The dishes we have match our style and home. A napkin and then the cutlery are added at each plate. The final step is placing name cards to match our seating plan. The table is ready for guests. The table prepares us for what is next.

The table we set for ourselves in our lives must be balanced too. The table we will create is a Life Plan. It nourishes, fills and satisfies. It's an experience like no other. Simply divine.

What we put on our plates, matters. There are essential elements in life that bring together a nutritious and delicious experience:

🍴 **Relationships:** We need relationships to thrive and feel connected

🍴 **Everyday Living:** We need to live with intent and purpose, find meaning and joy

🍴 **Health & Wellness:** We need to care for our emotional, spiritual and physical health

And when we connect these life elements to our money, we have a plan for living. Our table is set. So let's begin.

Starters and Appetizers

TASTY TIDBITS: SUCCESS

"The measure of achievement is not winning awards. It's doing something that you appreciate, something you believe is worthwhile."

—JULIA CHILD

You can smell and taste success in the kitchen, the scent of a delicious three cheese lasagne, an apple rhubarb pie or fresh bread baking in the oven. Success in the kitchen happens when everything comes together. Whether it is a dinner party of a meal with your family or just for one, the room has proper lighting and ambience. Our table is warm, inviting and inclusive. Everyone is welcome. The menu is balanced. Each item on the menu is carefully prepared using only the finest wholesome ingredients. It satisfies and nourishes us and our guests. The meal has a beginning, middle and end. Everything is well thought out and timed sequentially, as easy as 1, 2, 3. We are never left wanting more and leave the table fully satisfied.

Success in the kitchen starts with having a well thought out menu and a plan. The first item on the menu is the starter or appetizer. Appetizers are a delicious beginning to any meal to stimulate the appetite for the foods to come. An appetizer's purpose is to provide a little nourishment until the main course is served if there is an extended period between guests arriving and dinner. And, if there is any trouble in the kitchen, they create a time buffer to turn things around. Appetizers may be served hot or cold and eaten without utensils. A well-chosen appetizer will fit nicely with your main meal and wine pairing.

Can I offer you a mouth-watering stuffed cherry pepper, wrapped prosciutto, spinach and asiago dip with artisan bread or smoked salmon and cream cheese?

The history of appetizers dates back to France, centuries ago. Most cultures around the world have their own distinct type of appetizers. For example, the ancient Greeks and Romans sampled bits of fish, seasoned vegetables and olives, while Renaissance Italians served rolls or grilled veal.

The Pressure Cooker

To whet our appetite today, I want to serve you some tasty tidbits called successes. We have tasted them before. Success in life can be delicious. Each of us is already successful in our lives whether we believe it or not. Success comes in bite-sizes, small morsels that fill us up. We may have good jobs, nice homes, lots of friends and a close family. Or we may be stuck in jobs, don't live where we want, have lost connections to our friends and family, and search for more. This is a temporary situation.

Most of want more out of our life and seek greater success. But success has to bring us joy or it doesn't fill us up. When we live with purpose and intent we create meaning in our life. This makes us happy. But how do we create purpose or intent that creates the meaning we seek?

Bad days come and go but success is a powerful force that pushes us even further in life. Success for most of us is not the big kind, like fame or fortune. The success that most of us achieve in our everyday life may be a smorgasbord; a bit of everything through our relationships, health and wellness and living with meaning every day. All of these contribute to a successful life and feelings of accomplishment.

Success can be tangible or reflect a financial outcome, our home, career or material items. You can easily see it. Success can also be intangible or a non-financial outcome such as feeling good, taking better care of our self or spending more time with friends and family. How we define success or what it means to us is something very personal and can only be defined by you and based on what you value.

Each of us is at different stages in our life and therefore, has different values, needs and wants. The markers for success will be up to you. Success for me has always felt like the joy of winning a lottery minus the money. It's a feeling more than something tangible. I once jokingly shared with a friend how I felt that I had "won the lottery in life." She responded in a terse manner by saying, "Life isn't all about money." I agreed, and added that the feeling I felt had nothing to do with winning a lot of money. 'Winning the lottery' was a metaphor for the happiness I felt in my life. Most of us believe that money defines our success.

Many of us are feeling the pressure to be more successful in our lives. We may feel we don't measure up to some ridiculous idea of what it means to be successful woman today. For example, the pressure to make more money, climb the corporate ladder, find the perfect mate, have the perfect children, live in the right neighbourhood etc. You get the picture. What's important? What gives us meaning and creates joy?

Yet, the pressure to be more successful we feel is real and can seem like a pressure cooker. It comes at a price if what we seek offers little meaning or brings little joy. The pressure is so intense we feel we can't breathe. We feel trapped, much like food stewing in a pressure cooker. We begin to doubt ourselves. We may self-sabotage and engage in negative inner chatter about why we aren't more successful in life or why our career hasn't had the trajectory we envisioned. We may question our decisions because we lack intent, meaning and joy in our lives. We blame our money or lack of financial resources for not giving us more joy or happiness.

Women, in particular, have more demands on them as they seek to balance careers, family, home life, and relationships. The idea of 'having it all' is ridiculous. We can have it all, but it all might not happen at the same time. We have to become comfortable with this idea. I have yet to meet a woman who has everything she wants and needs. It's impossible. I have met women who I considered to be wildly successful yet they are unhappy. They may have career success but lack nourishing relationships or have allowed their health to evaporate. I have met women who have found wild financial success only to lose it and find it again. Their life is a roller coaster.

Achieving success is not a linear path. Think about Julia Child and her journey to find success. She started out as a copywriter. She followed her husband to Paris, France only to end up as one of the most influential chefs in the world. Her success took time to simmer and get to a boil. The challenge all of us face is that we want success now and are not willing to wait or we may lack the patience or discipline to let our lives unfold naturally. It's much like the difference between drinking instant coffee or freshly brewed coffee. Instant coffee is easy to make. It's quick. It's convenient. It takes less then two minutes to boil the kettle. The taste is just okay. However, brewed coffee takes longer to prepare and a few more steps. You can't compare the taste. The flavour is rich, pure and delicious. Scrumptious. Satisfying.

There is no disputing the fact that money and power are symbols of success. With money you can buy anything you want and have greater control over your life. But does this bring meaning and joy? Women who live on fixed income or the working poor will tell you that more money would bring greater joy to their lives. For many of us though, more money isn't the answer to what we lack or the gaps we seek to fill in our lives. More money won't make us happier or bring joy.

Yet, women still earned $ 0.77 cents for every dollar that men earned in 2012, according to new data from the U.S. Census Bureau. In 2012, the median annual earnings of American women working full time year-round was $37,791. American men earned a median income of $49,398. The gender wage gap between women and men has stayed at about seventy-seven cents on the dollar for women since 2007.

If money is a symbol of success, women are behind. Many of us will spend a lifetime catching up only to find ourselves needing 21% more money in retirement and having 30% less than men in our retirement funds. The numbers don't add up but life sure does add up! A successful retirement in the future depends on having money today to invest. Without financial resources, many of us will spend a lifetime living with fear and worrying that we will not have enough money in retirement. Some of us may buy into the idea of the 'Bag Lady Syndrome' of being homeless and penniless in retirement.

Arianna Huffington, the media icon and founder of the Huffington Post, has started a movement called the *Third Metric* where she is engaging some of the most powerful women in North America to help redefine success in our lives beyond the traditional symbols of success, money and power, into something that reflects our times. Money and power don't necessarily resonate with many women in the same way because success for many of us can't be measured with uni-dimensional metrics. We define our self using broader, non-financial measures. We find joy in being mothers, friends, co-workers, aunts, sisters, grandmothers, entrepreneurs, small business owners or employees. Put in a different way, we find joy and happiness in our relationships, how we live every day in good health and emotional wellness.

Today, more and more of us are looking to redefine success in our lives and find more meaning. We crave more because without meaning and intent that brings true joy, success feels hollow.

When we live our lives with intent and purpose, this creates meaning. With meaning in life, we can easily find joy. It feels real and authentic, much like us or good food. It has no preservatives, additives or modified ingredients. It's wholesome, natural and pure.

In my twenties, I defined success using the traditional symbols of money and power. Power manifested itself through having choice and control over my life. Money was an important marker of success and I achieved this by finding a good job, earning a good income and buying my first home. In my thirties, I defined success by finding a life partner whose values aligned to my values, building my family and finding a family home in a family friendly community. As I look to my future, I will find success that feels right too but there is no question that I will find greater success by living with greater intent and purpose because I won't be satisfied with less. The notion of success continues to evolve with greater emphasis on my health, wellness and relationships.

Life Can Taste Good

Success in the kitchen is easy to see and taste. Food either tastes good or it doesn't. It's simple. Each of us knows the moment when a meal is perfectly prepared. Our guests are silent at the table. They take in every little morsel and wash their palates gently. Cooking disasters in the kitchen are easy to see and taste. It's an awful experience and one surely not to be repeated. In our life, success is a desired outcome in all of our goals and activities. We are an accomplishment-based culture. Failure isn't an option for most of us. We accept it, learn from it and hopefully, don't repeat it.

Our time together would be well spent figuring out what success really means to each of us and what we are willing to do to achieve it. In your everyday life, what does success really mean to you? How would you define it? It is really easy to take a very narrow view of success but if we take the time to really think about it, we would benefit from thinking about our life more broadly. Every day, each of us experiences small successes that must be celebrated: passing an exam at school, getting a promotion, losing two pounds or saving $50.00. Success comes in all shapes and sizes.

Let's get cooking and start by opening up your pantry doors and looking at what's on the shelves and in the cupboards. You may be surprised what you find. Are all your shelves bare or fully stocked? Are there items in your pantry that are no longer useful or are past the expiry date?

Let's take a few moments to look through our life cupboards and how we feel about where we are today and our successes.

Food For Thought

Stop the cooking timer and reflect on your life. Unpack it bit by bit, like unpacking a bag of groceries. Remember, there are no right or wrong answers to the questions. Spend some time thinking about the successes you have had up to now in your life. How does it feel? What, if anything, is lacking? I've added my own example answers to a goal, after the questions below, to help get you going.

1. How successful do you feel today and why? How do you define success in your life?

_____

_____

2. What accomplishments are you most proud of or give you joy?

_____

_____

3. Do you aspire to find more success? What would it look like? What joy would more success bring to your life?

_____

_____

4. How does money and power play out in your life? Do you buy into the idea that they are metaphors for success in society?

_____

_____

Here is a peek into one of my goals.

My Book Vision: It's June, 2015. My new book is published and people are enjoying it. This is a bite-size success for me, then something pretty extraordinary happens. My new book, *Food For Thought: The Joy of*

Living a Delicious & Nutritious Financial Life, reaches the New York Bestsellers list because women have connected with my message and approach to finding more joy in life. I could only have dreamed of this success. I have achieved a very big goal and it feels great. My financial resources have taken a boost for the better. I have more money for retirement, travelling and starting another home renovation project. I have more time to pursue activities that provide meaning in my life. This is victory. This is my success.

The Main Course

RELATIONSHIPS: FRIENDS, FAMILY AND COMMUNITY

"Dining with one's friends and beloved family is certainly one of life's primal and most innocent delights, one that is both soul-satisfying and eternal."

—JULIA CHILD

Having successful relationships, matters. It is a sign of having a successful life. It has relatively little to do with money or financial resources. Having relationships with people that matter contributes to our success on many levels. We find comfort and inspiration in our friends and family. Friends boost our emotional wellbeing, support and encourage us to grow and to become better people. We make lemonade from lemons.

There are many fine ingredients that make up successful relationships with friends, family and our community. Successful relationships are like a good meal. They are authentic and real. I have close relationships with my neighbours. They live far enough away for privacy yet close enough if I need to borrow a cup of sugar, flour or other cooking essential. This gives me comfort.

In the countryside, extended families are so important because they provide much needed emotional and financial support. Living in a small community has its benefits. It's almost a given when you live in the country that you get to know most of your neighbours. There is a level of connectivity and trust because we have built strong relationships. We depend on each other. This differs from living in a larger city where connections can get lost. People are too busy and lack trust in strangers. Slowly the small town or community is dwindling away. Recent research suggests, for example, that in Canada, eight out of ten people live in large urban centres. With the demise of the small community, will our connectivity to each other fade?

Cooking For One Is Little Fun

Globalization is making it possible to experience other cultures and communities, real time, 24/7. We are becoming more connected and finding ways to become global citizens, but this can't be mistaken for close relationships. Being a global citizen means we have a broad and open view of the world; understand the vast dichotomy of different regions.

In life, sometimes the best places are those yet to be discovered. Low cost airlines and charters offer cheap travel to virtually anywhere. Travel is often one of those wonderful experiences that bring joy and a lifetime of memories. Many people can afford to buy a ticket to some place new and exciting. It is much easier to pack up and move to a new country, further a career or retire.

Technology is changing how we live beyond the kitchen. It is increasing our efficiencies and helping us to expand our knowledge and understanding. The world has become much bigger and yet much smaller.

Our kitchen is the hub of the home and a place for entertaining, doing homework, cooking, and socializing. It used to be a place just for preparing meals.

The kitchen is evolving. Technology is transforming the space and making it more modern with state of the art appliances, tools and machines. For example, state of the art fridges are being developed that have full functioning virtual dieticians. A dietician in the kitchen will coach good eating behaviours, monitor our diet or caloric intake and make suggestions. They will help us achieve weight loss goals and encourage healthy eating habits.

Wouldn't it be great if each of us could have a virtual assistant in our lives? We would get so much more done and feel less exhausted.

Many countries have experienced an influx of new immigrants from all over the world as they look to start a new life, build relationships and contribute to the community. We can experience food from all over the country in our own backyard.

For many newcomers in a city or town, it may be challenging to find meaningful relationships and like-minded friends. It can be lonely in a new town. Social opportunities may be closed off, making it difficult to assimilate and build new connections.

Our careers are taking so much more from us we have little time to socialize with family and friends. Demanding and successful careers require a time commitment at work, also known as "face time." In order to find greater success professionally, many of us must work longer hours and commute. Workplace relationships have become more prevalent because we are spending so much time at work and not as much time at home or socializing with our friends. This is not fulfilling. It can't be. However, many workplace relationships do not have the same ability to fulfil or create the deep meaning we seek. Most are short-lived and many of us find ourselves searching for connections. We may experience career success and make a lot of money. But it's lonely at the top.

With the diminishing connection to community and growth of the online world, many of us are losing the benefits of close, deep and meaningful relationships. A study was published late 2014 in the *Personality and Social Psychology Review*, which indicates that many of us are most likely to thrive with well-functioning close relationships. These relationships could be romantic or with friends, parents, siblings or mentors.

Dr Brooke Feeney of Carnegie Mellon University in Pittsburgh and Professor Nancy Collins of the University of California at Santa Barbara said "thriving" involves five components of wellbeing.

These include "hedonic wellbeing", such as happiness; "eudaimonic wellbeing," having intent and meaning in life as well as progressing towards life goals; and "psychological wellbeing," such as the absence of mental health problems.

Relationships matter more than ever. Researchers conclude that "social wellbeing" provides deep and meaningful human connections. Positive interpersonal experiences as well as physical wellbeing are necessary to thrive.

Sometimes relationships can go sour or from hot to cold. Things can become very bitter. No amount of sugar coating will sweeten it. Here is a story about Carol, one of the guests at our table. Most of us would think someone at age twenty-four would be starting out in their life. But her journey was to start *over, and* began with living a life that was misaligned to her values, goals and desires. By every account, we would think this young woman had it all: education, job, home, car, money, and an upcoming wedding. We may be surprised by her story and outcome.

Carol was twenty-one when she became engaged to John. They were high school sweethearts and followed each other to the same university. After the first year of university they moved in together. They both completed their degrees around the same time. Carol was first to finish. She secured herself a wonderful job at a technology firm and found herself a rental apartment in downtown Toronto. Life was good. She had lived in the suburbs all her life and Big City living was fresh and exciting. John followed her to Toronto, moved in with Carol and found a job, but not as successfully as Carol. This created an imbalance in the relationship and unhealthy behaviours.

After a year of living together, Carol realized that the relationship wasn't working for her. She felt constrained, held back. She was on a different path than John. He wanted to get established quickly and move forward at a young age to live his parents' or potential in-laws' lifestyle. He was set to repeat the formula: marry young, have kids, a house in the suburbs, a dog and car. He didn't know that he had fallen into the trap of 'keeping up with the Joneses.'

Carol was frustrated. She wanted to experience life, travel, but felt trapped. With their aggressive financial goals, they lost sight of living and enjoying their twenties. Carol had goals of travelling more and running marathons but they all required she spend time and money on things that mattered to her. These did not materialize. Her goose was cooked.

Carol knew she had to do something but felt emotionally stuck. She had spent the last seven years, one-third of her young life, with John. One Christmas Day, John suddenly proposed to Carol. She said yes. For the next year she tried to convince herself this was the right move for her. Others told her she was too young to marry. She needed to find herself and explore life possibilities while she was young. She didn't really listen because she felt trapped and was so far down the path with John she didn't know how to get out.

As the wedding approached she became more uneasy about her decision to marry. The year living together revealed more differences and misalignments in goals and values. There was no balance. It was all about financial goals: saving more money, not spending, long term planning. John did not know how to enjoy the here and now. John had become the centre of her world and she lost connection to friends and her family along the way. A recipe for disaster.

Carol's emotional wellbeing was low. She had lost a very important ingredient to living a successful life. One day she woke up and realized it was time to change. She had outgrown her relationship with John. She was just going through the motions of getting married because, doesn't every young woman dream of her wedding day? Carol broke off the engagement. At twenty-four, Carol started over again.

Carol was burned by this life experience. She experienced a large financial loss. She returned the engagement ring, cancelled the reception hall, stopped production on her wedding dress, cancelled the honeymoon tickets, gave up the joint car and split the furniture. When the relationship was over, she kept the apartment she was living in because it was the one piece of comfort and stability she had left.

Her savings had also taken a beating because she had funded most of the entertainment costs because John earned less than she and was stingy with his money. The latter part of Carol and John's relationship was like a really bad and long meal or a really bad scene at the dinner table or restaurant. You can't wait to get out. This story may have stirred up a lot of emotion in you. How many people have been in relationships where this was the case? Sadly, I suspect many.

The upside to Carol's financial loss is she will recoup her expenses. She has time on her side. This life event taught Carol some very important lessons. While John was in Carol's life he took much of her energy, emotional and financial resources to meet his needs. This left her feeling empty and hungry for more. Lucky for Carol, she found the courage and strength to walk away and start fresh. She is slowly rebuilding relationships with friends and family and through this experience she has realized their importance.

She spent the year following her breakup exploring the possibilities in her life. She created a Life Plan and set new goals. Carol started slowly to make changes. Each time Carol experienced a mini-success, those delicious bite-sized morsels, she took on more. Her confidence built. Carol is back on her feet again. She lives with intent and has found meaning. She is joyful. She is running marathons, travelling with her friends and dating again. She is cooking with gas.

Cooking from scratch allows us to select the best and finest ingredients and prepare recipes our way. It gives us the opportunity to enrich our self and make us into a new person. It's our recipe and no one else's. Many women will find themselves starting over in their thirties, forties or fifties. This could come about through lifestyle changes, embarking on a new career, widowhood or divorce. We can find inspiration from Carol.

At each stage of our life there are distinct events and rites of passage and some of them are not necessarily about our age. Perhaps you may be experiencing a life event right now.

Family and Friends Give Us Comfort

We eat comfort food such as mac & cheese, pizza, spaghetti, French fries or hamburgers. When it's cold outside, a warm cup of hot chocolate warms our tummy and lifts our spirits.

Comfort food has the ability to lift our spirits and make us feel better in the short term, but over the long term, we might gain weight and acquire health challenges.

Friends offer comfort to us. They have the ability to nourish and enrich our lives. There isn't a better life experience than the one I am experiencing today with women at my table, breaking bread and sharing personal stories. Getting together with friends is a traditional pastime our parents engaged in. The meal doesn't need to be fancy. It could be potluck or a smorgasbord. It is such a simple pleasure, connecting, laughing and celebrating the joy of living.

Friends have become more important than ever in this ever-changing world. There are many different types of friends, including those we spend time with, enjoy their company, but do not lean on for emotional support. These are friends that we may share many mutually enjoyable activities with, but everyone likes to keep it light. They are like a piece of cake.

Friends have always been important in our lives. As children, we made friends and generally kept one or more from elementary school. While in junior or high school, we typically expanded our circle and found one or two more friends who have stayed with us for life. While at college or university, we may have also found new friends. This is our circle of influence. It's real. It's authentic.

There are special friends or, our *Go-To* friends. They are the crème de la crème. They are the ones who are always there for us and never judge us for who we are. These friends are like a hearty bowl of potato soup on a cold winter day. These are friends we need to be emotionally available for us. These are friends we will seek for emotional support and advice and expect to receive the same in return. These friends will tell us when they think we are going off track and when they think we are wrong.

Some relationships are long and fulfilling. Others are short and non fruitful. The Chinese believe that we should begin and end any relationship in our life the same way. In other words, if we find our self about to end a relationship or move on, give it the same dignity and consideration as when we started it. Most of us end relationships poorly because of hurt, disappointment or breach of trust. We must be mindful of our feelings and act with grace even if those around us don't.

Women often volunteer and are active in the community. Whether it is sitting on non-profit boards, adult-supervision for school trips or managing our kid's local team sports. Our homes are in communities, which connect us to each other.

Friends and relationships matter, and so does our involvement in the community. We can find deep and nourishing relationships in our communities when we engage with other like-minded women whose intent and purpose are the same as ours. Imagine what happens when we get a whole bunch of hockey Mom's together to work on a task. We have the ability to cook up a storm with ease and confidence.

I have been volunteering in my community for the past thirty years. I started working for the Canadian Cancer Society as a canvasser and eventually became a manager. I spent time volunteering for the Heart & Stroke Foundation. Volunteering my time and services is important to me because not only does it offer opportunity to give back to the community in a meaningful way, but it also connects me to organizations I value. This gives me purpose, creates more meaning in my life and results in joyful living.

Here is a story about my volunteer experience. When I took on the role as team manager for my son's hockey team in 2013, I had no idea the amount of work that was required to effectively manage a team! I already had a demanding career and balancing home life sometimes posed its challenges. Given I had never managed a hockey team before, I thought the task would be straightforward.

How difficult could it be to manage a kid's minor hockey association team? Well, let me tell you, it was an eye-opening experience. Sometimes it felt like scrubbing pots for hours and hours. Other times, it felt like drinking a skinny latte, delightful.

There is so much to coordinate, including scheduling make-up games, booking tournaments, planning fundraising events, working through team politics and making sure parents and the kids were content. It was one of the greatest experiences of my life. It helped that my husband was the coach so we often shared team responsibilities, but his job was coaching and mine was managing the team. Not only did I get to participate in my son's hockey life, my social circle grew.

As a mentor for the Forum Women Entrepreneur, I work with other like-minded women who are trying to grow their businesses. We share deep and profound learning experiences with each other. We have busy schedules and must ensure our time together as mentor and mentee doesn't eat up all our time, energy and resources. We have to be efficient and productive when we meet.

While working in Retirement and Financial Planning, Private Client Group, BMO Bank of Montreal, I was the lead for our United Way events in 2011. I made it a point to set up events that allowed us to actively engage with our community. We participated in events such as Meals on Wheels, delivering food to people in Toronto who were old or not mobile. We experienced heartfelt gratitude at every stop. We saw people thriving in our community and how our volunteer dollars actually were used. It was eye-opening. There is personal satisfaction in having one's feet on the street and giving to people who have little or are not capable of independent living.

As I embark in a new role with The Canadian Women's Foundation on their leadership fundraising team, I will be mindful of the things I have learned from my volunteer work. I will think smarter, ask more questions and hopefully find the same joy I have experienced from past volunteer experiences. I look forward to working in the community and helping women, while also strategizing with other like-minded women in the board room on how we can drive fundraising, create greater awareness of the benefits provided by the foundation, and find simple ways for people to contribute financially to this worthy organization.

Food For Thought

1. Think about your family, friends and community. Who offers the greatest meaning for you? Family life today is dynamic and ever-changing. How important is your family in your everyday life? Who are you including in this? Is there anything going on in your family right now that could keep you from growing? Have you created a wall around yourself to keep past family hurt away? What would you change in your current family situation?

_____

_____

_____

2. How is your circle of friends? Do these relationships fill you up or drain you? Who is your sweetest friend and why? Who can you call to grab a cup of coffee or meet you for a quick glass of red Bordeaux? Are you the one always calling up friends to get together? Are there friends in your life that you have outgrown? If your circle is small or lacks the support you need, how do you think you could grow your circle of friends? Where could you connect with other liked-minded women? Do you have a particular hobby or sport you enjoy where you could meet new people?

_____

_____

_____

3. What are the three things you are grateful for in your relationships?

_____

_____

_____

4. Think about your volunteer time. Are you using your volunteer time well? Is this the right time in your life to be volunteering or do you have too many family or work demands that need your attention now? Are you using your skills in the best way possible? Is there an organization that you would like to volunteer with? Why is this organization important to you? Is there a way you can give back that works with your schedule and responsibilities?

_____

_____

_____

EVERYDAY LIVING

"This is my invariable advice to people: Learn how to cook—try new recipes, learn from your mistakes, be fearless, and above all have fun!"

—JULIA CHILD

Living with a clear purpose every day will allow us the ability to find meaning and joy everyday. Just like we need food to nourish us and keep us strong and healthy, we must nourish ourselves in what we do each day. Work is part of our daily life. Work can be paid employment or taking care of children or family. It can also be volunteering and being active in the community. All offer rewards and satisfaction if they are closely aligned to our values. Many of us want to escape the grind and go somewhere new and exciting where we have a purpose, feel valued and appreciated, and live with joy. But how?

Every day I stop the cooking timer to reflect on what is good in my life. This is gratitude. I think about how I am living my life, whether my activities and pursuits align to my values and what really matters to me. I plan my day carefully. I am deliberate in how I spend my time and with whom. Time has a way of melting away. The weeks go by. The years go by and all of a sudden we look around and think, How did I get here? We search for more meaning in our lives. We question almost everything and feel we have been sold a bill of goods. The daily grind consumes much more than our energy. It takes a piece of us and leaves us feeling empty. We show a brave face to the world but inside we are melting away.

If I didn't pay attention to time, I could spend the entire day cooking and trying new recipes. How would I ever pay the bills? I choose carefully what I stock on my shelves and how I load my pantry. Because my plate is already full, I am careful not to fill it with things that won't nourish and fill me up in favour of food that is rich, dense and full of nutrients.

Many of us lack purpose and are not finding meaning in our lives. But if we are living a life that makes us unhappy or are working in a job that is not satisfying, everyday living will feel like a grind. If we engage in activities or work that is unfulfilling, like eating junk food, life will lack meaning and intent. We will feel malnourished. Empty. We will crave other things to appease our hunger and quench our thirst.

This is Janet, another guest at our kitchen table. She shared with us the daily schedule of her sister who is a busy woman. She has purpose and finds meaning in what she does daily, but lacks direction on where her life is going. Here is a story many of us share with Janet.

The Plate is Already Full

We get up at 6:00am, shower, dress and head to our kitchen. We grab a coffee; maybe make our lunch or lunch for family. We get everyone organized and ready for school. We walk the dog and then take out the garbage. We run to catch the commuter train, pull files or our handheld from our bag. We answer emails, check our calendar. Our stop arrives and we get off the train and briskly walk to work and are the last one in. We spend our day in meetings, running errands at lunch, grabbing a bite to eat while doing errands or at our desk. At the end of the day we race out of the office to catch the train. We are exhausted but keep going. We sit on the train going through emails our boss sent after we left. Our mind wanders aimlessly.

We wonder if we took something out of the freezer for dinner. We rush to pick up the kids from school or daycare, start dinner, check to see if there is clean laundry and throw in a load or two. We start helping the kids with homework then eat dinner and out we go again to take the kids to their activities. Drop them off and run to the grocery store where we grab some things for the next few days since we can't think beyond mid-week. Race to get our kids and get them home and organized for bed.

Finally, a moment to ourselves. We crash on the couch, check our emails again and start to wind down. It's 8:30pm. We have some ME TIME but are too tired to think, so we drift into mindless TV and eat chips. We wake up only to realize its 11:30pm. Time for bed.

Sound familiar? We crave for more. We secretly ask our self, Is this all there is? We question our life and choices.

The plate is full and in fact, it is over–flowing. We have little time for our self. How we spend our time and what we do, matters.

Variety is the Spice of Life

There are health benefits to using spices when we cook. Spices can enhance the flavour of any food taking the most boring and making it extraordinary. Spices don't obscure or hide flavour at all. When our day is filled with mindless activities that gives little intent or meaning, living is not joyful. We need to spice things up. We drag ourselves out of our beds to get going. Our day starts first thing in the morning and finishes when our head crashes on the pillow at night. And, for many us, it continues through the night in our dreams and unfortunately, for some of us, through vivid nightmares. The latter leaves us drained and tired the next day but we push on because we are women, after all. This is what we do.

Variety is the spice of life but it can be easy to get a little lazy in the kitchen, particularly if there is no one to cook for or if you are super busy. I enjoy simple pleasures. A simple pleasure for me would be buying a new cookbook for twenty dollars. I will get years of enjoyment from this small purchase. I can spend literally hours in a book store, moving from one section to the other. There is so much positive energy and I am inspired to do more, learn more. When I find myself in the culinary section, my emotional wellbeing skyrockets because I am in a creative environment with endless possibilities. I feel at home.

Eating home-cooked meals offers the greatest potential to eat healthy and fill our bodies with the right nutrients. We know exactly what we are cooking or baking. We choose the recipes we want and buy the best ingredients we can afford.

I recently purchased *Jaime Oliver's Food Escapes.* It was first published in 2011 and I suspect there have been changes since. I bought the book in the first place because of the front cover. Jaime is in a rustic setting somewhere in Europe and I was immediately drawn to the book because of this image. Further, when I touched the matte cover it was so tactile and gritty. I loved the feel of it, like lightly crusted food. I sat down in my marvellous kitchen and started flipping through the pages. The images and recipes sparkled and they drew me in. I felt as though I was in the same places and on the same journey as Jaime. I wanted to try all the recipes.

At first I was overwhelmed with the amount of choice in my new cookbook—it had 359 pages! The task was almost daunting. Where to start? I realized I needed to temper my enthusiasm and think through the best approach to tackle this new and wonderful book of culinary delights. I searched for one or two recipes that really stood out. I wasn't looking for the same old, same old. I wanted to stretch myself. Grow in the kitchen. Would it be best to try something new for my family or to create something for an upcoming dinner party I was planning? This gave me *Food For Thought*. I needed to pause and reflect, and stop the cooking timer.

I was drawn to the section on Paris, France. The desserts were magnificent. The World Famous Tarte Tatin was accidentally created by two sisters who prepared the tart and left it in the oven too long so they turned it upside down to serve. They didn't know what to expect. It was a stellar success. The sisters turned a kitchen nightmare into something incredible. A bite-size success, of course. How many of us have had our own version of Tarte Tatin?

Chefs are creative and remarkable in their craft, along with a big dollop of ingenuity. The kitchen can teach us wonderful qualities for living.

We must learn to open our self up to life's possibilities. Sometimes we can close our self off, like an unopened can on a pantry shelf.

There is always a simple answer to our problems when we look closer at them. I realized the best immediate use for my new Jaime Oliver book was to find a recipe that called for available or fresh in-season produce. What was my mindset? How did my mood come into play? In the kitchen, emotions and moods, matter. Did I fancy anything in particular? I checked my dinner party log to make sure I hadn't prepared something similar before. Foodies want to make sure we don't serve the same thing twice unless our guests insist we prepare something we have made before. It's etiquette. This gave me clarity and direction. I decided that my family would be the best test for trying something new before I made it for guests. There is pride in the kitchen and ego too!

Who would ever have thought that buying a cookbook would create so many questions and result in so much research, reading and exploring? Two hours and twenty minutes later, I found the perfect recipe and carved out time later in my daily calendar to enjoy more of this cookbook. I had more pressing matters to attend to.

Much like in everyday life, it is easy to get swept up in the culinary world. I could easily spend a day or week sorting through new recipes, researching new books and trying new recipes. But, alas, my time is limited, and I could go broke doing this! I have learned to think smarter in my kitchen. Food is a necessity of life. It nourishes and enriches my family. Money is well spent cooking nutritious meals and making my family happy.

Stopping the cooking timer is the best way to pause and reflect how we are living on a daily basis. If you are like me in the kitchen, you may find yourself consumed in activities that may not be fruitful. Our daily routines, matter. They keep us focused and grounded. When we choose activities that offer intent and meaning to us, we have joyful days. If we engage in activities that are not, the days feel like cleaning up in the kitchen after a big dinner party or being the dishwasher in a commercial restaurant.

Chefs plan ahead. Successful people plan ahead because if we leave life up to chance, random things may happen that don't offer much joy. It's important to be selective in life. In the grocery store I am absolutely selective about what I put in my basket. Where we choose to work, live and the people we socialize with, matters. All of them can contribute to a joyful life, much like cooking does.

French Fries are my Favourite Comfort Food

Food offers comfort. Our homes provide comfort. Home may be a house, apartment, a room, or a boat. It doesn't really matter where home is. Your heart is where you decide your home is. You always take your heart with you. Our homes give us permission to be at home with ourselves –'home sweet home.' There is something so grounding about our homes. Our home can have a big influence on our everyday living. Living in the country is peaceful and quiet, but commuting to the city is long. Living in the city offers many amenities, but traffic is awful and it's noisy.

If our home is nourishing, we will thrive. If it is draining, we will feel gloomy. It is legacy, and one of the most important places in our life. We define ourselves by where we live. Older people often don't want to move out of their home because it offers so much meaning, joy and history.

When we return to our childhood home, it is amazing how we are transported back in time and perhaps to a simpler world. We feel a sense of connection, belonging and community. Yet for some, we feel no connection. We conjure up bad memories and a sense of not belonging.

I have lived in many different cities and homes, and my old stone farmhouse in the country by far offers the most nourishing environment. It doesn't matter what I look like, how much money I earn, or what I do for a living. None of this is relevant or has any meaning.

Whether you own or rent, feeling a sense of belonging and having connection to your environment is important to living a balanced life. A home can give you feelings of pride. Some believe that home ownership may be a rite of passage, a signal they have grown up. But it is also expensive to own a home. Yet, the average home prices in North America are climbing such that home ownership is becoming unattainable. For many people, the financial commitment is far greater then renting or leasing. People who live in Paris mostly rent. They can't afford the high price of real estate. Years ago, I stayed at my best friend's aunt's flat in Paris, only to find ourselves sleeping in closets that were converted into couchettes. The apartment was only 250 square feet but was in the heart of the city, walking distance to fine shops and restaurants. Finding a good apartment is incredibly difficult unless you check the obituaries, a strategy used often in New York City.

Bricks and mortar build a house. It's not the structure of a house that defines it as "home," rather, the emotional attachment you may feel. But for many, home ownership continues to be a dream and goal. Living in a big house, with empty rooms and a big mortgage, can make you feel empty. Living in a small house may make you feel restricted and confined. Finding the right balance is essential and you must think about what is right for you.

Where you choose to live, matters. Most of us want to live in the best neighbourhoods we can because they will have the best schools, shops and amenities. Spending three hours a day commuting will not enhance your everyday living. Walking to work in fifteen minutes will shorten your commute and give you more time to do other things. Home affordability and commuting are issues to consider. Find what is right for you.

A big city may offer more amenities but it may offer less community. A small town may offer more community and connections but less amenities. Figuring out what is right for you is important because attaching to your home and neighbourhood will make you feel connected to something. I have lived in the city, country and in the suburbs. At each of my life stages I have desired something different.

Think about where you are living today, your home and surroundings. Why are you living here? Is it close to work or family? Do you like where you live? Does your home give you comfort? What is missing? What would you change? How well does your home suit your life right now? Have you outgrown it? Think about your future. Where do you want to live and why? How close will your friends and family be? How important is that to you?

_____

_____

_____

The Triangle in the Kitchen

Well laid-out kitchens have just the right amount of space between the cooking, prepping and cleaning areas—the 'work triangle.' It connects the three work areas of the kitchen: the cleaning area or sink, the cooking area or stove/oven, and the refrigerator. The space between them is ideally about three feet and some believe it can't be greater than seven feet.

If the area is too small, it is cramped and a cook won't enjoy her time in the kitchen. She will always feel constrained. If the area is too big, it will be cumbersome and difficult to work effectively. If space is not well designed in a kitchen, sometimes moving a wall or closing an opening is an easy renovation solution to make the triangle better. This is no different in our lives. If our personal space is not configured well, it won't feel right. Making a change will probably improve it. But sometimes we just can't see a solution to our problems.

Each of us has personal space in our home, office or someplace else. The kitchen in my old stone farmhouse is my space. It's a place that brings the best out of me and brings people together. It's configured well. When I first bought the farmhouse, my kitchen was small, a cramped space where really only one person could work in it. I was terribly frustrated with the configuration. When I took out an adjacent wall the kitchen grew to twice the size. I took two useless spaces and made them into one big functional space.

Think about your home and your personal space. How does your personal space fit into your home? Do you have a place where you can find some peace and quiet time? Are you happy there? If yes, what is it about your space that you love? What, if anything, do you want to change? What does your space mean to you? Do you feel safe? Is your space an oasis of calm or chaos? If it's chaos, how do you want to change it?

_____

_____

_____

Hungry for More

It's easy to get burned at work. Some of us may find ourselves in the hot seat working in jobs that consume most of our calories, leaving us feeling empty and malnourished. In North America, we have become a work-obsessed culture. The impact our jobs have on our lives may not be healthy and take its toll. I have yet to meet a woman who doesn't feel the struggle of balancing work-life.

Here is a story about me and how I made some big changes. It was not that I was unhappy in my life but I wanted more and had a profound need to give back to others. My everyday life was excellent, but it was time for me to make a change. It's best to make changes when things are good versus when things are bad. Your mindset is much better. I had to go against the grain and do what no-one else around me was doing.

One day in 2009, I looked out my Bay Street window and pondered life in Toronto. Another year had passed in my corporate job and I knew there was something amiss. I had this feeling there was something holding me back but I just could not say what. There were no tangible barriers. I had a very good job as Senior Manager in Retirement and Financial Planning, Private Client Group, BMO Bank of Montreal. I reflected on my life and realized that it was time to reignite a goal from the past to help me make a big change. I tried to fast forward and think about where I would be in five years. The vision I had for myself wasn't good.

We must always keep our eyes peeled on the future. Much like having an emergency kit in the kitchen that includes vinegar, soda water and spot remover, we must also plan ahead in our lives and have emergency kits. This includes saving money for the rainy day emergencies in our lives and getting the proper insurance to fit our personal situations.

In my search for answers, my life was about to make a 360 degree turn in 2009. I decided to pursue a Masters in Business Administration at Western University.

My friends told me I was crazy—going to school full time, working and managing a family? I didn't let their comments hold me back. My time as a student was filled with mini-hurdles and challenges. I spent the eighteen months of my degree trying to balance a major shift in my time. School obligations took priority and some months required that I spend days or weeks away from home. My domestic partner took over many home responsibilities and together we successfully managed this life transition.

I spent the first half of my degree working full time. This was a recipe for disaster. My employer was generous. They agreed to let me reduce my hours to part time, which I continued for the duration of my degree. I balanced and juggled, every day and every week. I was fully dedicated toward achieving my MBA. I was living out my dream. I am proud to say that graduating with my degree in 2010 was one of the best things I ever did in my life. Going back to school changed my life forever and opened doors to greater possibilities. I didn't realize how stuck I was. My direction was clear and I was in charge of my life.

With my newfound knowledge and accomplishment I had reached a milestone in my life and found the success I was searching for. Most of all, I wanted to use what I had learned working in the corporate world of business and finance to help women improve their lives. And, equally important, the changes I made later created the perfect conditions for quality family time and the ability to be actively engaged and involved in raising my family.

Many of us hold on to a dream or goal for years but never fulfill it. My philosophy is to never leave a recipe half baked. We may play with the idea of pursuing it but often find reasons or excuses not to move ahead. But something pretty amazing happens when we do fulfill on a goal we set for ourselves in the past. I fulfilled a goal that lay dormant for twenty years. My emotional wellbeing got an enormous boost with this accomplishment and it transformed my everyday life. I found greater meaning in my work and found the success I was seeking. All of this contributed to being a better person and having better relationships.

Each of us may have the yearning to make change—to find more, to change jobs, buy a new home, and renovate the kitchen—something that will bring us more joy in our life. Confidence in our life comes from having a plan and knowing where we are going and having a series of small successes or quick wins to propel us forward.

Women are becoming the major bread winners in many families. With this, comes a new set of circumstances. The majority of women today work in the labour force and participate in the world economy. It is inevitable that money and power will define women in the same ways that men have traditionally been defined. For many women, success goes well beyond the idea of money and power because relationships, personal wellness and everyday living, matters too.

Recent research released by the Journal of Health and Social Behaviour called "Gender, Job Authority, and Depression" revealed information that gave me *Food For Thought*. In brief, the study found that depression symptoms increase in women as they climb the corporate ladder. They note that "Broader social factors and cultural beliefs related to gender and status affect interactions in the workplace and make job authority more stressful for women compared to men. In the current cultural climate, women's confidence and authority are viewed less favorably than men's." What this means is that women in authority positions deal with negative social interactions, negative stereotypes and prejudice, and resistance from subordinates, colleagues, and superiors. The study also found that women in authority are evaluated harder compared to women in less authoritative roles or men in similar positions. The impact of this puts stress on women and impacts their health.

For some of us, we may be paying far too high a price for our career success. With too much emphasis on the money we may neglect the things that really matter to us. What price are you willing to pay for your career success?

We must have gainful employment to pay for bills and essentials, but what price are we willing to pay for career success? Many of us struggle with this. We love our lifestyles and don't want to change much, even if our jobs are draining and unfulfilling. A change in job or lower salary may jeopardize our lifestyle. We are willing to trade off having lifestyle and material items for working in jobs that don't mean much to us and bring little joy. In the long term, this is a recipe for disaster. It's not a sustainable model and I guarantee you it will change for the worse. You will become disenchanted. You will become someone you don't like or even recognize. I saw this first hand.

The desperation to be successful or to succeed in work can result in people engaging in negative and self-serving behaviour. Here is a brief story of a woman I know. She is very successful, has a senior title, power and authority. She is a sophisticated dresser and can buy anything she wants. She is earning money well into the six digits. She drives a company car and travels exclusively in business class. Her success is to be admired.

Yet, she is not a nice person. In fact, she has a reputation of lying and telling half-truths. She has climbed to the top by stepping on all those around her. She discredits her peers and subordinates only to elevate her status. Married with no children, she lacks an understanding of the working mother's plight. Although it appears she is well regarded by people outside her organization, she is not well regarded by her staff or other leaders. How does she sleep at night? Women like this make us feel we never measure up, but in fact, we are better. How many of us know of someone who will do whatever it takes at all costs to climb the corporate ladder?

In 2012, Professors Linda Duxbury and Christopher Higgins surveyed 25,000 Canadians in their "National Study on Balancing Work and Care Giving in Canada." Their findings revealed that many of us are overworked and this is causing pressure and tension in us, impacting our emotional and physical health and wellness. "Almost two-thirds are working more than forty-five hours a week—fifty percent more than two decades ago. Work weeks are more rigid, flex-time work arrangements have dropped by one-third in the past ten years and to top it off, only twenty-three percent of working Canadians are highly satisfied with life, half as many as in 1991."

Women's financial needs are also shaped by their desire to balance family with career. Many take time off or work part-time when they start a family, weakening their financial position. Even when women choose to focus on a career they often face a wage gap compared to their male counterparts.

The research uncovered some other important points which you may already know about because it is your reality every day.

🍴 We struggle to find balance working and taking care of children.

🍴 We take work home with us, taking time away from family. We are putting in approximately seven extra hours a week working at home.

🍴 Many of us are losing sleep and not taking care of our health and wellness. Almost one-third of the respondents said they felt overworked and drained of their energy.

Michelle Obama stated in an interview in 2013, "I personally know the challenges of leading a busy life at work and at home, trying to do a good job at both—and always feeling like we're not quite living up to either—and trying not to pit one against the other, really trying to balance it . . . I call myself a 120-percenter . . . If I'm not doing any job at 120 percent, I think I'm failing."

Work-life balance is a struggle for women but it doesn't have to be that way.

Let me introduce you to Amanda, here at our table. She took charge of her life and career to get on the right path. She found herself in a real pickle several times and got burned but was able to reinvent herself every time to find the success she was looking for.

Amanda was in her mid-twenties and found herself starting over again. She married at twenty-two and divorced three years later. This was not her plan or goal and she moved back home to live with her parents. To get back on her feet, she took an entry level job at a well-respected multi-national in Toronto, Canada. She started to learn to stand in her strength. After a few years, she was ready to re-enter the dating scene. She learned from her first marriage the importance of shared family values and having common interests.

She wanted to marry again and build a family. She enrolled in a local cooking class hoping to find someone who shared her love for food. She didn't want to leave this up to chance and took the initiative to orchestrate this part of her life. She was successful and met a young man who was also looking to find a life partner. They were aligned on many levels and were married a few years later. As she blossomed in a stable home life, she was ready to take on the bigger challenge of kick-starting her career.

Up until that point, she had held entry-level positions and wanted more. She set a goal for herself to advance her career and knew the only way to achieve it was through more experience and education. She wanted to go to business school to earn an MBA and created an action plan for success.

She engaged with Human Resources at her workplace to learn more about her employee benefits package and what educational assistance was available. Her plan was generous and covered post secondary education. She wrote the GMAT or standard test for business school and scored high, and subsequently applied to several universities in Toronto. She was accepted and enrolled in a part time twenty-four month MBA program. Her employer requested she sign an agreement that she would stay with the company for five years after graduation.

She had to spend weekends and evenings working on her courses away from her family plus worked full time. It was a recipe for disaster because it strained her domestic relationship. Her parents worried about the lack of balance in her life and stepped in. She took an interest-free loan from them to help cover her living costs. She successfully completed her MBA and eventually found the corporate success she sought. She is now a role model to younger women in her organization.

The good news is, many employers are responding to the need for greater work-life balance for employees, as long-term effects of overload and lack of balance affects work performance. Many researchers have studied the evolving issues connected to overwork and lost community connections. While the implications of an unbalanced work-life are numerous, they all share a common outcome: Living an unbalanced life where work dominates our time can be detrimental. Long or stressful work hours can cause problems with our heart, blood pressure, sleep cycles and much more.

In addition, stay-at-home moms who do not receive formal pay from work may have trouble valuing their time. In 2012, Time Magazine published an article on the value of the work of a stay-at-home mom. Their findings were clear: Stay-at-home moms put in a work week of 94.7 hours, worth an average hourly rate of $17.80 or $112,962 per year. This takes into account all their responsibilities: cooking, shopping, cleaning, organizing the family's activities, educating, and personal care.

If you are a stay-at-home mom and know how time flies because you are always busy, you will not be surprised by this. Make no mistake, your time is of tremendous value to your family and to society.

Is Your Work Simply Divine?

For most of us, our working life defines so much in our lives and our identity if we let it happen. "I am my work." has become all too common a phrase. It is our livelihood, source of financial security and stability and consumes most of our waking hours. We define ourselves by our jobs, titles and salaries. So much of our self-esteem is tied to our work. That's the conclusion of a survey in 2012 of more than 100,000 Americans conducted by the Gallup-Healthways Well-Being Index. It says 16.6% of unemployed Americans are depressed compared to 5.6% of those who work full time.

There are emotional and financial benefits to working. "Self-esteem and self-worth are closely aligned with working," says psychotherapist, Charles Allen.

Having a job means so much more then we may realize. Self-esteem and pride come from being a contributing member of society. We typically don't engage in actual conversations with our self about being contributing members to society by working outside of the home, but it is intrinsic, nonetheless. Ask yourself why you work. Is work providing you the fulfillment you seek? If no, why? What small thing could you do differently or change that could have the biggest impact on your career or job?

Being employed helps us feel wanted and that we're contributing to our finances, according to psychotherapist, Elizabeth Lombardo. It also gives us social support—"a buffer against depression."

The reality for many of us is we are stuck in jobs or careers we have outgrown that offers little meaning or joy. Only one-quarter of Canadians are happy and satisfied with their work because of the strain it is placing on their lives. Recent research tells us that many of us are stuck in jobs that make us feel negative. We lack engagement and search for more. It may require some reinvention or going back to school. Action is required. A plan is needed.

Have you ever dreamed about becoming a chef or opening up your own restaurant or Pied-à-Terre? A career in the culinary world could be life-long. There are many roles you could have for a full and enriching career. Culinary schools offer programs that are tailored to the role someone seeks. To become a chef, most people will need at minimum, four to five years of formal schooling. Tuition can cost $15,000 a year for a total of $60,000.

Food For Thought

Think about how you spend your time every day. Whether you are employed full time or part time, work from home or don't work in traditional paid employment, think big picture about your life. Think about daily life and whether it fulfills your needs, gives you intent or purpose.

1. How does your work and life phase compare? How does your job or career bring you joy? Are you in the process of looking to reinvent yourself? What are you looking to accomplish in your career or job?

_____

_____

2. Are you at the beginning, mid or nearing the end of your working life? Do you feel you are just collecting a pay stub? How does money play out in your work? What are your primary goals for working? How do you feel about where you are in your work life? What would you change? What needs to happen to make that change a reality? Do you have your dream job? What, if anything, is holding you back from attaining it? Do you seek more money, position or responsibilities? Are you being paid what you are worth? Are you in the right career? Do you look forward to getting up and going to work every day? How could you find more joy in your work life?

_____

_____

_____

3. In order to make a change in your career or take on a new role, there may be a need to upgrade your skills or to go back to school. Think about education in the context of lifelong learning. Most of us learn new things every day from reading, taking courses and sharing stories. What gaps do you have in your education? Do you want to go back to school to finish a program or start something new? What additional education, if any, do you need to get to the next level? Do you really need more education to advance or are you using it as an excuse to cover up lack of confidence, fear or other emotions that may be holding you back?

_____

_____

_____

3. What are the three things you are grateful for in your everyday life?

_____

_____

_____

HEALTH & WELLNESS

"Moderation. Small helpings. Sample a little bit of everything. These are the secrets to happiness and good health."
—JULIA CHILD

Good nutrition and having a balanced diet are the best ways to promote good health and longevity, but health and wellness goes well beyond having a balanced and nutritious diet. When we think about our health and wellness we need to look at it more broadly such as our physical, emotional, mental and spiritual wellbeing. Having good relationships boost our emotional wellbeing and contribute to a successful, healthy and happy life. Family and friends make us feel full and nourished. We need them in our daily lives. How we live every day impacts our emotional wellbeing and personal wellness. When we live with purpose in life, we find meaning in our life. This creates joy.

Health is the Best Form of Wealth

Without health, not much else matters. There are an abundance of health, nutrition and wellness experts in the market today. I encourage you to make your health a priority and get informed. There are leading experts whose advice is making a difference in the lives of people. Dr. Oz has become a very popular source for information related to increasing longevity and personal wellness. The Mayo Clinic offers some of the best advice in the world around preventative health care. Both have websites with rich information. I encourage you to learn more about your body, the impacts of aging, diabetes, blood pressure or other chronic diseases and how stress may be impacting you.

Research shows that wealthy people generally live longer because of better nutrition, less anxiety, more time for friends and family—all things that contribute to contentment. They have the financial resources that allows for more and better choices in how they spend their time and with whom. Yet, they may or may not be happier than people with fewer resources. But when we nourish ourselves, no matter what our financial status, everything comes together socially, emotionally, physically and spiritually.

Let me introduce you to Susan, sitting at our table. Her life appeared to be bubbling along quite happily as she managed her full plate which included two school-aged children. But she still searched for greater joy, fulfillment and success and one day realized that her life was passing her by.

Susan is a stay-at-home Mom. Like most moms, over the years she put family first and herself second. Both her children were at school full time. One day she decided it was time for a change in her life. She was disenchanted with her body image. Her pre-maternity clothes no longer fit. She needed a makeover. Susan had put on weight with her two children and was motivated to lose it and feel better about herself. She wanted to earn money to help contribute financially to her family. What held her back before was the lack of personal time and the ability to make herself #1.

When Susan reached her late thirties she realized it was time to set a new direction. Lucky for Susan, she had a spouse who was supportive and he motivated her to take better care of herself. She enrolled in Pilates at her local community centre and started working out four to five times a week. She was committed to reaching her goal of losing thirty pounds.

Susan lost the thirty pounds and returned to her pre-baby weight. She splurged on buying new clothes to fit her new slim body. She traded in her dated hairstyle for a fresh look and image. Susan did not invest a lot of money to recharge her life. She did require some financial resources to fund her fitness classes, attain her accreditation and to start up a small business that had little to no overhead expenses.

Today she has a thriving business in her community and is able to balance work demands during the day and be available for her children before and after school. The ability to free up time for herself has made an enormous difference in Susan's life. She is happier, feels good about herself and the financial contribution she is making to her family. She feels less dependent on her partner.

Many of us may be healthy but may feel that our emotional health is not where we want it to be. We are exhausted, tired, stressed, and worry about our lives, money and our families. The worry epidemic is taking its toll on us. We may seek to find more comfort in our daily lives. Many people are turning to spiritual healing approaches such as yoga as a way to combat stress and find inner calm. Others are turning to the church to connect on a spiritual level.

Food for Thought

Let's go back to your list at the beginning of the book. Where does health and wellness fit in? Feeling good about our self and the choices we make every day for ourselves, matters. When we think about our health and wellness, many of us will take a narrow view and only think about our physical health. But our health also includes our emotional wellness. When we don't take into consideration our emotional health, we may weaken ourselves. We become more susceptible to seeking out comfort food to feel better. We may start to spend money to fill voids in our life. We may buy 'pick me ups' to feel better and get into a cycle of spending money mindlessly. In the short term, this may not be detrimental, but again, it is the cumulative effect that can cause problems.

Each of us seeks comfort, from our homes, food and money. A peanut butter and jam sandwich is one of the most sought-out comfort foods. It is readily available and the good news is, peanuts are chock full of protein, fibre, unsaturated healthy fats, thirty essential nutrients and an excellent source of vitamins and minerals. It's good for us. For those of you who have peanut allergies, yogurt covered raisins are a great alternative.

Think about your wellness on multiple levels—physical, emotional, and spiritual. Expand your thinking about what you really need. How are you feeling overall? What changes do you need to make to be healthier? What are you doing today that is really working well and you want to continue? What are you doing that may be working against you?

Spiritual:

_____

_____

_____

Emotional:

_____

_____

_____

Physical:

_____

_____

_____

A la Carte Menu

CREATE A MENU JUST FOR YOU

"Upon reflection, I decided I had three main weaknesses: I was confused (evidenced by a lack of facts, an inability to coordinate my thoughts, and an inability to verbalize my ideas); I had a lack of confidence, which cause me to back down from forcefully stated positions; and I was overly emotional at the expense of careful, 'scientific' thought. I was thirty-seven years old and still discovering who I was."
—JULIA CHILD

A la carte items are served in addition to a Prix Fix or Table D'hôte, or featured menu. This added selection is usually for the picky or fussy eaters. Some of us would be quite happy with the featured menu. Our palates are diverse and distinct. But others, unfortunately, do not have the same luxury. A la carte for us today will provide additional considerations and more selection in the context of our Life Plan because life offer's limitless possibilities.

TRIED AND TRUE RECIPES

Some of us may be excellent home cooks. Others may not be into DIY or do it yourself and prefer ready-to-eat or takeout. When we stick to tried and true recipes we can almost predict the outcome. When we try something new, we can't predict the outcome but we can ensure greater success through preparation and planning. Tried and true recipes stand the test of time. We know what to expect and if something goes wrong we can respond accordingly.

There is always a risk of setting lofty goals in life and in the kitchen. The way to minimize the risk is to take a "test and learn" approach. Many of the most famous chefs in the world have test kitchens where they try new recipes before they go commercial or serve up dishes to patrons in a restaurant. In the test kitchen, chefs learn and adjust recipes by adding more spices, salt, pepper, butter, garlic or may have to deal with their own 'Tarte Tatin experience.' They manage the risk through feedback and adjust as needed.

Most chefs don't start their careers in a five star restaurant. They start much lower in status and responsibility, perhaps as sous-chefs or even a dishwasher. Many chefs have had previous careers. They may be on their second, third or even fourth careers. Who said you had to stay in one career your entire life? For example, Julie Child never set out to bring French cuisine to the American public. In fact, she started her career as a copywriter in New York City. She only started cooking when she was in her late thirties. Whereas Jaime Oliver, another renowned chef, knew early in life he wanted to become a chef. He dropped out of high school to enter culinary school at age sixteen. Two very influential chefs in this world came about their career and success differently.

Goals can come in many different shapes and sizes. We may already have a good sense of what we want to accomplish in life. We may already be well on our way to achieving our goals. Or we may need a gentle nudge. There are constraints like time and money. We may face road blocks or obstacles that almost seem impenetrable. In the kitchen, time is the biggest obstacle to overcome because cooking is a creative yet methodical process that can't be rushed.

A Life Plan consists of a series of goals, usually three major ones that can be executed simultaneously. It also depends on what the goals are. For example, you may have two goals in mind. You may want to purchase a new home, and get into better shape. Both of these goals can be accomplished simultaneously. The first goal will require an aggressive savings strategy where the other goal will require time.

Creating a vision for ourselves is essential because it acts as a catalyst, like flour and water, to help us reframe our thoughts and feelings so that our actions drive us towards greater success with ease and confidence. We may have some very specific things in life we want to accomplish. An action plan will bring everything easily together.

Before we go any further, I want to acknowledge and applaud you for sticking with me. Take time to reflect and review what we wrote together in this book or the thoughts that came to mind as we continue.

Life Stages

There are many stages to cooking. The two most important stages are preparation and cleaning up. Over time, many of us will learn to cook by heart and follow recipes that we love and others enjoy. Many of us are still figuring out what we like to cook in the kitchen or trying new recipes to broaden our menus. It can be daunting to try new recipes. Cookbooks offer a wonderful way for us to try new things. Over time, once we have been cooking for years, everything just seems to come together with little effort. Life is no different. Time is needed to let life unfold naturally.

Each of us will have a different starting point or life stage. At each stage of our life, there are distinct events or rites of passage that are not necessarily related to our age. For instance, we might be having a child in our forties in a second marriage, rather than in our twenties or thirties. We may be starting a new career in our forties or fifties. There are no predefined parameters of what needs to happen at a certain age. Age matters in the sense that it is a guide post only, so don't get hung up on it.

Your life is not about watching water boil. It's about rolling up your sleeves and getting messy. The temperature of the water must be just right because you don't want to scald yourself with impulsive decisions or ideas that are half baked. Bringing water to a boil involves a complex process. Navigating through life is complicated, yet chock full of endless possibilities and choices. Consider the following four life stages. Where are you?

1. Starting Out

2. Getting Settled

3. Getting Established

4. Transitioning to Retirement

HEAT UP: STARTING OUT

Starting out is like water heating up and getting ready to boil. Most likely, someone starting out for the first time is in her twenties. She is probably in her first real job—not that working in the summer during school wasn't a real job. At this stage, someone may have left home and is truly independent, paying rent and utility bills. There may be many firsts—first real relationship, first job, first home. At this stage, many women will try to figure out where parents/guardians and family fit in their life. Friends will be very important and most of the spare time will be spent entertaining. These years tend to be more optimistic; when everything in life seems to begin.

Much of our time in our twenties will be about finding our self—our identity. We may be experimenting or trying new ways of doing things. We will start to understand our values and what really matters to us. We will start to have more confidence in your decisions because they will start to slowly reflect your life values or what matters to us. We, no doubt, have had some success in life and have accomplished goals.

LOW BOIL: GETTING SETTLED

Getting settled in life is similar to achieving a low boil on the stove. Moving from starting out, we transition to the years of 'settling in'— in jobs, homes and relationships. We may find ourselves in a partner relationship, maybe with kids, or maybe not. We may start to feel the pressure cooker of life and the demands that come with maturing. We may have had some early success in our career and are cautiously optimistic about our future. Our life may not be unfolding as we want. We may have put some of our goals or dreams on hold we set in our twenties. Family and career demands may be squeezing in and we start to search for balance.

Our job may be taking more of us then we are willing to give. Or it exhausts all of our energy and when we come home we have little to give to those we love. We start to venture into uncharted territory and might be feeling a little uneasy with all the changes in our life. We may think to ourselves, Where am I going? or we may think, How did I get here?

We probably now have a pretty good idea of who we are. Our value system is in place but we may be challenged to be living by our true values. We have had some setbacks in life. We may be carrying some personal 'baggage' we want to let go.

FULL BOIL: GETTING ESTABLISHED
When life is moving in the right direction we are on a boil. We know who we are and what we value. We may be a little skeptical and disenchanted with work. Our career may not have had the trajectory we planned. We may be looking to make some big changes in our life—divorce, go back to school or switch careers. We may find ourselves in a second marriage, juggling the demands of a new set of children in our home. The demands of family may take priority. We may have less time for ourselves and put things we want to do or accomplish on hold. Aging has become a concern for us. Our health may be suffering from stress and we know we need to take better care of ourselves. We may be asking ourselves, Is this it? We search for more. We begin the cool down process and let life unfold.

COOL DOWN: TRANSITIONING TO RETIREMENT
As we transition to our late fifties and sixties in life, we will start to shift our focus towards one of the longest periods of our life, retirement. For many of us, retirement will be like a pot cooling down or a sweet dessert, pastry or cheese and crackers, delights we have earned at this stage of our life. Follow on to the next section called "Dessert" to learn more about retirement and how to enjoy these years!

Engage Sous Chefs in the Kitchen

Some believe that too many cooks spoil the broth. In goal setting or Life Planning, this is not always the case. Engaging others in our decision-making process is practical and smart. We must also consider the important people in our life. In commercial kitchens or restaurants, the more people the better. 'Many hands make light work.'

Many of us may have families, children or partners. We may wish to engage them in this process early on because some of our goals may be family goals or include other important people in our lives. A family that sets goals together accomplishes more. If we find our self with family or partner-oriented goals, we may want to take the lead and map them out.

If we keep personal goals or dreams to our self, we may inadvertently create a barrier with those close to us. We need to figure out how much information we can share without feeling vulnerable. It's damaging to our self-esteem to announce a goal to everyone around us, as it can create undue pressure

Multi-Tasking in the Kitchen

Multi-tasking is at the heart of commercial kitchens around the world. Staff are trained to perform many duties at once. The key to success in a commercial restaurant kitchen is to work as a team, with staff chipping in wherever needed to make sure the customer is served and content.

Multi-tasking can be an effective strategy to get things done. Our brains are designed to handle many things at once. It is not always considered a dangerous activity but we can overload our self with too many things. It depends on how much of our cognitive resources are being used. Some activities consume more resources then others. For example, talking on the phone while driving takes up a lot of our awareness, making us distracted and dangerous on the road.

Many of us multi-task in our lives and have multiple goals we are working on simultaneously. It really depends on how much emotional and financial resources are needed for each goal. Much of our life requires us to achieve many goals at the same time. Spend time figuring out how much time is needed per goal and make sure you have enough hours in the day to accomplish your goals. This risk is about taking on too much and spreading your self too thinly. Prioritize goals based on the ones that have the biggest payoff or benefits to finding more joy in your life.

Both men and women multi-task. Research indicates that neither gender is better at it. Some recent research would suggest that men and women are good at multi-tasking different kinds of activities. What researchers have found is that men and women's brains are wired differently. Most of us would agree that each gender excels at doing different tasks.

Food For Thought

Over the past chapters we worked through some thought-provoking questions to stimulate our thinking. Many of us may already have a set of goals underway in our Life Plan and now might be a good time to record what they are and to reflect on the progress made. Remember your goals are different from your daily To-Do list or activities. They are broader in scope but your To-Do list may have a step you need to take towards accomplishing your goals. For others, we may want to get cooking by creating a Life Plan and articulating a series of new goals. Whatever your starting point is, you are on the right path.

Here is a list of some specific goals women have shared with me. See if any of these resonate with you or whether you could add your own goals to the list:

🍴 Losing weight

🍴 Eating better

- Buying a new home/renovating/down-sizing

- Going back to school

- Finding a new job

- Getting a promotion

- Finding a mentor

- Buying a new car

- Boosting self confidence

- Getting fit

On the following pages is a worksheet for you to use. It offers some very specific questions to answer about your Life Plan and goals. Specificifty is the essential ingredient in a Life Plan. You may find you have multiple goals. The challenge becomes prioritizing them. You can multi-task goals, but keep them to a maximum of three at a time.

Cooking up a Storm in Your Life: Action Planning

GOAL #1 *(be specific)* BIG PICTURE LIFE GOAL

_____

_____

Where does this goal fit into my Balanced Scorecard? Health & Wellness, Everyday Living or Relationships?

_____

_____

Where am I in my life? Starting out, getting settled or getting established?

_____

_____

What is my timeline? (be time specific)

_____

_____

What are the key steps I need to take? What small change could I make that would have the biggest impact on my goal?

_____

_____

What will my goal cost?

_____

_____

Who could help me achieve my goal?

_____

_____

How will I stay on track and not lose sight of this goal?

_____

_____

How will I know I reached my goal? What will success look like?

_____

_____

What qualities do I need to exhibit to achieve this goal?

_____

_____

How much time do I need to allocate weekly to achieve this goal?

_____

_____

Example #1: Action Planning

Goal: Lose 20 pounds before my sister's wedding in June

🍴 Where does this goal fit into my Balanced Score Card? Health & Wellness, Everyday Living or Relationships?

Personal Wellness

🍴 Where am I in my life? Starting out, getting established or getting settled?

Growing in my thirties. I just had my first child and want to get back to my pre-baby figure.

🍴 What is my timeline? (be time specific)

6 months before my sister's wedding.

🍴 What are the key steps I need to take? What small change could I make that would have the biggest impact on my goal?

Start exercising 2x a week.

Walk to work.

Eat more nutritiously. Stop snacking on chips.

🍴 What will my goal cost?

I will need to spend another $15 a week on more nutritious and healthy food, for example buying blueberries, strawberries and fresh food. But I will save money because I won't be buying chips and snacks.

🍴 Who could help me achieve my goal?

I could get a personal trainer or attend fitness classes at my local YMCA. Maybe one of my girlfriends may want to join me and we could create a buddy system to motivate each other.

🍴 How will I stay on track and not lose sight of this goal?

I will keep track of my weight loss on a chart. I am motivated to lose weight because I am in my sister's wedding party. I dislike having pictures taken of me and with this extra weight, I am horrified. The camera puts on 10 pounds. I have to lose this weight to fit into my bridesmaid dress.

🍴 How will I know I reached my goal? What will success look like?

I will feel great walking down the aisle of my sister's wedding. I won't feel embarrassed. In fact, with my new found figure, I may even start to enjoy having my picture taken.

🍴 What qualities do I need to exhibit to achieve this goal?

I need to commit and show up every day. I must be consistent and disciplined. I know how I get when I come home from work. I am tired. I get a bit lazy. I order takeout.

🍴 How much time do I need to allocate weekly to achieve this goal?

I will need to allocate at least 2 hours a week to achieve this goal. If I work out 4 times a week for 30 minutes this will hopefully be all I need.

Dessert

RETIREMENT

"Find something you're passionate about and keep tremendously interested in it."

—JULIA CHILD

Everyone looks forward to what's on the dessert menu. You may want something sweet and yummy or choose to have fruit and cheese but my experience suggests that most of us are usually satisfied at this point, and have little room for more food.

We grow up learning that we can't have desserts or sweets if we don't finish our main course, but children will bargain for their dessert even when they don't finish their entre. They will tell you that they have an extra stomach just for dessert. They will use anything in their drawer to get you to let them have dessert. In life, it is no different. Retirement is like dessert, and can be sweet or bitter. Thinking about retirement well in advance will help you to have your just desserts your way.

If you are like many women today, the thought of retirement planning might seem far away as you struggle day-to-day to manage your family and finances. But for Boomers, retirement is just around the corner or has arrived. The good news is that research tells us that many women are looking forward to retirement. Given that women are living longer, many of us could spend over one-third of our life, twenty to thirty years, in retirement. The bad news, according to retirement planning expert, Moshe Milevsky, is that women will need twenty-one percent more money than men in retirement; much of it for healthcare expenses not covered by typical government pensions.

We may be already making some lifestyle adjustments as we get more comfortable with the idea of retiring and no longer working. We probably have more energy than when we were working. We may be planning to fulfill some long-held dreams. We will also be thinking about such things as our estate and creating a personal legacy. We finally have time to give back to the community.

These years are about creating joy, meaning and intent in our life. At the same time, we want to be carefully monitoring our health issues. Prosperity of the soul becomes a driving force. The needs of women in the retirement corridor are very specific with key considerations in life issues. For some of us nearing the retirement corridor, our thoughts may be shifting away from traditional paid employment to our golden years. We may be thinking ahead, but we haven't got a clear vision or we can't articulate our next steps.

Although we can't orchestrate everything in our life, planning to live a long life is smart. Starting the conversation today will lay the bottom pastry for future action-planning. Given retirement could be one of the longest phases of our life, we need to embrace life-planning strategies. By visualizing our future and creating our Big Picture, transitioning into the next thirty or forty years will be easier and more enjoyable.

Most of us dream of the day when we will retire, often when we are having a bad day at work. The thought of lounging on a beach or playing golf comes to mind, with all its personal freedom. But the reality is, if we are like many Canadians today, the thought of retirement may be a far-fetched dream as we struggle with life, family and finances. We may have a lot of pent-up fear, anxiety and uncertainty about it.

We want to spend our later phase living a worry-free lifestyle. We may have created some kind of retirement plan but have we really taken the time to think about what our life will really be like and what we will be doing?

If we are in your late fifties and early sixties, we are probably starting to wonder if we have saved enough to retire or if we will have to continue working. This is a big question and for many of us who have not saved enough money, continuing to work will be a reality. Our work life will be extended not because we want it to but because we have to. For others, the thought of giving up our professional career is a daunting and frightening concept. We have defined ourselves by our career and now without it, what will we do for intellectual stimulus? For many in their late sixties, lifestyle is top of mind. We can only play so many games of golf. Many in their seventies and eighties tend to think more about creating a personal legacy.

Many women I met who have successfully transitioned to retirement have been planning this transition for a while and have figured out how they will spend their time and where they will live. They have been cooking up their retirement by getting themselves into the right mindset for what is ahead. Here are five steps to help you cook up yours:

1. **Visualize how you want to spend your time.** What do you like to do? What makes you happy? Do you have a hobby or activity you used to do and wish to recapture? Or will we continue to consult or start the small business you dreamed about in your working years? How will this fit into your big picture now?

   _____

   _____

2. **Consider all the important people in your life.** Do their needs and plans fit with your vision of the future? For example, you may have new grandchildren who you want to see as often as possible but living half the year away may make this more difficult.

   _____

   _____

3. **Think about how your health may impact your Big Picture.** Do you have health concerns that could affect what you will be doing and where you will be living in the future? Having access to good medical care will be paramount in your decision-making. For example, retiring to your summer home may have been the dream but how about the local health care support? It might not offer what you need. Perhaps have a back-up plan?

_____

_____

4. **Take stock of your current living arrangements.** Most people want to grow old in their homes. It offers continuity and familiarity. Will your current home age with you or will you have to make some changes? Perhaps you'd prefer to retire in a different country or climate? What impact will this have on your healthcare or distance away from your family?

_____

_____

5. **What is your time frame and financial situation?** The most important consideration is timing. Will you be retiring at the same time as your partner and friends? If they continue to work for several more years, how will that affect you? What are the financial considerations and funding needed for your aspirations and dreams? A retirement financial plan will help you pull it all together. All major financial institutions in Canada offer retirement financial planning services as well as independent firms. Learn more about the value of expert advice later in later chapters.

_____

_____

Tools in the Kitchen

THE CAST IRON SKILLET: MONEY

"The only real stumbling block is fear of failure. In cooking you've got to have a what-the-hell attitude."
—JULIA CHILD

A cast iron skillet was developed to last a lifetime in the kitchen. We never throw away a skillet. For centuries, cast iron skillets have been passed down from generation to generation. A skillet can stand the test of time. It requires care. Experts believe that skillets must avoid water, soap or any harsh cleaning ingredient.

Our money is the cast iron skillet in the kitchen. It's a metaphor to describe how we use money. It's a tool we use in our life to help us achieve our goals.

Money helps us cook our Life Plans and goals fully. This is the stage in our experience where we bring together our goals or recipes and get our cast iron skillet working for us. A cast iron skillet is one of the top ten cooking tools for the kitchen and falls just behind the paring knife. We need it to sauté, simmer, and fry. Imagine how limited our cooking would be if we didn't have it. In the same way as our life would be limited without money. Some of us may not be using our financial cast iron skillet to optimize the cooking experience. Now is the time to get this tool working for you to help you to achieve your goals you set in your Life Plan.

Money is a tool in our life and we have to use it correctly. Some of us may not have been shown how to use a cast iron skillet or our money.

Let's fix that. But money alone will not bring us a joyful life. If we put all our eggs in one basket and think our money trumps relationships, everyday living and health and wellness, we will have less than a baker's dozen. Money fits into our lives. It's a financial resource for life and measuring our success. Retirement savings, little debt or an emergency fund are signs the cast iron skillet is working. Without money, we can't effectively execute on our goals or Life Plan. Money is a tool to buy comfort and lifestyle and to help us reach our goals. Our goals are usually about accomplishing a task or activity and rarely about financials.

Stop the cooking timer and take a look at your Life Plan you created. Add up how much money you will need to achieve your goals. It may be daunting or overwhelming. You may wonder how you are going to be able to achieve your goals based on your income, savings and other financial obligations. We will figure this out together. For example, a goal may be to buy your dream home. The financial goal may be to save more money, get a low interest rate mortgage or pay off your mortgage quickly.

We can use our money, literally and metaphorically, to over-indulge on chips, chocolate or other snacks that are not good for us. Some of us don't have a healthy relationship with food. We may drink too much coffee, eat too many fatty foods or not drink enough water. We don't have a balanced diet and give in to our weaknesses.

Some of us don't have a healthy relationship with money. This applies to many people and not just people with limited financial resources. The very wealthy may not have a healthy attitude toward money, particularly people who have grown up with wealth, who think that money has no value. For someone who has little, money has much value.

Having a healthy relationship with food is no different than having a healthy relationship with money. Food gives us comfort. Money gives us comfort. We can waste food. We can waste money, eating out or takeout. Besides, nothing is more nourishing and good for us than a home-cooked meal. If we overspend and don't take care of our money we may not have enough for our short term goals or a comfortable retirement. How we spend our money today could have lifetime impacts on our financial health.

Let's take a quick coffee break and fill up our mugs. Let's think about ways in which we can improve what we are already doing with our money. There are some tried and true strategies we probably could do today that don't require a lot of effort. It might be something as simple as cooking at home more often and dining out less. Spending less. Saving more. Many celebrities prefer to dine at home because this gives them privacy and the opportunity to relax. There can't be anything more dreadful then slurping spaghetti or cracking lobster claws with a camera focused on you twenty feet away.

For many of us, it boils down to managing our cash flow to know exactly what we have or where our money goes. Most of us have no idea and this could be holding us back from reaching our goals in our Life Plan sooner.

Whether we have limited financial resources or have a lot of money, managing cash flow or our monthly disposable income (once our bills are paid) is essential. Wealthy people are equally challenged to manage their cash flow. Money can slip out of our hands so easily. And whether we like it or not, we need money. It is important. We have to embrace this notion but not let money rule our lives. More money means more opportunities to accomplish more goals in our life.

Too little or too much money can create pressure for us. If we have too little money, our lifestyle may not be that good. If we have too much money, people may constantly be asking for handouts. Money can create pressure for us. We may feel we don't have enough.

A pressure cooker is one of the most convenient and low cost cooking tools a busy woman can have because it does most of the work for her. A pressure cooker takes food, water and other liquids and cooks them all in one pot. It does not let any air in or allow liquids to escape. It's a fast way to cook a meal. The trapped steam increases the internal pressure and temperature. When cooked, the pressure is slowly released so that the pot can be safely opened. A pressure cooker can turn relatively inexpensive ingredients into a wonderful dish.

Yet, I have never used a pressure cooker and just the name of it makes my stomach queasy, like when I overeat or am under pressure. I prefer to cook using old fashioned and traditional methods such as baking in the oven, and cooking on the stove. I like to see what I am cooking, baste it or even add a few extra spices along the way. The pressure cooker does not allow for flexibility.

Sometimes money can feel more like a pressure cooker than a cast iron skillet! The pressure we feel to become more successful in life is similar to the same pressure we may put on our money to solve all our problems. It's a heavy burden.

Money evokes emotion. To fulfil our goals and dreams, our money must serve us and we must nourish and care for it. Most of us believe that more would make us happier.

But no one wants to work for peanuts either. Some of us may be in low paying jobs that barely cover our expenses. The money in/money out cycle is commonplace. We want to earn enough money to enjoy life's comforts and secure our financial future.

How does money play out in your life? Do you feel you have enough? It doesn't matter how much you have or how much you earn, most people feel they don't have enough. What one small change could you make with your money that could have the biggest impact?

Here is June, sitting at our table. She found herself in hot water with an unhealthy relationship with money. She overcame this by learning to see money in a new light.

June started over again in her forties. She spent a long time feeling sorry for herself after her marriage ended. Prior to her divorce, June's husband managed the family finances so she basically stepped away from her responsibilities to manage her money. She had a sizeable monthly allowance given to her by her husband for household expenses. Money was never a concern for her. She didn't have to account for how she spent it because her husband did not really care, as long as the home was looked after and dinner on the table.

Over time, June acquired disrespect for money. She really didn't care much about money because it didn't mean anything to her. She felt that the money was never really hers and she didn't value her contribution to the family. She lived in a financial pressure cooker.

After her divorce, June struggled with managing her money and made numerous errors. Each time she attempted to get a handle on her situation and started learning new terms or strategies, she found reasons to abandon the plan. Lack of time was her excuse. Her disrespect for money began to sabotage her in ways she never imagined. She got burned. When her mother died, everything came crashing down and she felt vulnerable and raw.

Becoming the Executor of her mother's estate forced her to engage with money. This added a level of complexity to her situation that she was not knowledgeable about at all. Most people don't understand the complexities of being an executor to a will. She really had no choice as she was an only child. Her mother left her entire estate to June, who now had money of her own. You think she would have been happy.

June was intimidated by money and the power it can have over us. Her husband had kept tight control of the money and allocated it to her as if she was a child. She woke up one morning and decided it was time to change. She wanted to get out of her rut and start fresh. She knew very little about the mechanics of money and how to make it grow. She started by creating a Life Plan and created three goals for herself. She eventually took her windfall to an investment advisor and began a working relationship with him. He knew her personal story and helped her create a retirement and spending plan.

For many women, a life event will trigger a change in behaviour. A sudden increase in wealth can often result in a person squandering the money if they don't have a financial plan.

June's journey to being more financially savvy was triggered by two major life-altering events: the breakdown of her marriage and the death of her mother. It was through these defining experiences that she was forced to change for the better. Many of June's insecurities surfaced during her marriage. She couldn't stew in the past but had to make a future life for herself that was fresh and delicious.

The Food Bank is Not an Option

We can be burned by divorce. There are emotional and financial impacts that can scald our heart, mind, and financial resources for a very long time. Divorce can create another challenging economic reality for women. Most of us don't enter into marriages thinking about divorce unless we engage in pre-nuptial planning. Most businesses start with an exit strategy or a plan for dissolution. In life, we rarely enter into anything thinking it will fail.

About one in five women fall into poverty as a result of divorce. Eight out of ten single parent families are headed by women, which add up to one million households in Canada. Being poor increases the likelihood that a woman's children will also be poor. Women are also likely to be single or alone in retirement, due to high divorce rates (the average age of divorce is fifty-six) and the tendency of women to outlive men.

Women who also leave a partner to raise children on their own are five times more likely to live in poverty than if they had stayed. The impacts of divorce on women are alarming and many women who divorce may need to increase their income twenty percent to thirty percent to maintain a decent standard of living.

Small Talk in the Kitchen

Spills, breakage, slips or falls can occur in any kitchen. That is why it is essential to have an emergency kit in the kitchen that consists of a fire extinguisher, baking soda, club soda, cloths for cleaning spills etc. A misfortune in the kitchen can also cause negative emotional reactions. Many of us have accidentally hurt ourselves slicing and dicing vegetables. Who hasn't spilled a glass of red wine on their favourite table cloth or carpet? It's devastating. Money can create a lot of emotion too—fear, shame, embarrassment. Managing our emotions in life is essential to feeling in control. Emotions are a natural part of our lives but how we choose to respond defines everything. Money can frustrate us, particularly when there never seems to be enough or we are not achieving our goals sooner because of lack of funds.

Our attitudes toward money will impact how receptive we are to changing, learning and starting something new. Some of us struggle just to address the here and now, never mind when conversations about our personal finances and futures need to be addressed. This mindset must change.

We may be carrying a lot of anxiety about our money and don't even know it. Most of us have the following experiences in common:

- Dealing with our money is stressful and can be overwhelming at times.

- We believe that nothing we do will make our lives better.

- We don't want to talk about our money today, or our financial futures, because it makes us uncomfortable.

- We have experienced several unpleasant outcomes with our money.

- Money is a symbol of success and power and our self-worth can be tied to it.

Dealing with money is stressful and can be overwhelming even for the smartest, brightest and most successful women. Money can be a barrier to women reaching goals, living with greater intent and finding joy. Bright women can be very confident in their work but under-confident about money. It's not easy to be confident about something that we know little about or isn't as exciting as cooking in the kitchen.

Some of us are not willing to change and feel that nothing we do will make our money situation better. Some of us have given up on our money. We just don't care about it. We may judge many people by what they do with their money, what they make or how they spend. Good role models are hard to find. Sometimes our friends can influence us to spend money we don't have or we want to have the same as them and spend money we can't really afford.

Talking about money often makes us uncomfortable. We don't want to talk about our financial future because it scares us. Getting older can create anxiety in women and men, particularly if we feel our lives have not unfolded in the way we thought. We can easily engage in short-term thinking but thinking about tomorrow seems too vague. Who can really plan ahead twenty or thirty years? It doesn't feel natural.

Talking about money is still a taboo even between the best of friends. Most people will share details about their money situation if they find common ground, establish trust and start the conversation about what matters to most of them, their lives. Many of us have no trouble sharing stories about the bargains we buy or the deals we get. We muse in these conversations. We can't wait to tell our best friends how much we paid for a new pair of shoes or handbag at the outlet mall. But the conversation will go no further than that!

There are many reasons why we don't openly talk about money to our friends, partners or family. For some of us, our family experiences with money were not great. Our parents fought about it, they did not have enough, or money was not handled well. We may not have been given an opportunity to learn about money. Research tells us that most families teach boys about investing and Bigger Picture issues such as economics and teach girls about managing the household budget. This misinformation and lack of experience can also lead to discomfort in discussing money matters.

Many of us don't understand the financial language used to talk about money. When people start talking about "dough," I think about baking in the kitchen. It's hard to engage in a conversation if we don't understand the language. Many financial advisors speak to their clients using jargon that is totally foreign to lay people and rather than appear 'stupid,' clients pretend to understand. Advisors often don't realize this important fact. They are not bad people, just maybe not the best in communicating in consumer understandable terms.

An unpleasant encounter with our money can leave us feeling less confident about our decision-making abilities. For example, a woman I know was told to buy strip bonds in her investment portfolio by her investment advisor. She knew nothing about strip bonds and asked her advisor to explain it to her. After several attempts to understand the mechanics of strip bonds, she still didn't get it, and left her advisor's office angry. She called a friend to help her "calm down." She was furious and felt "stupid" because she didn't understand how strip bonds work. She still doesn't understand the mechanics and has found that her advisor has invested her money in them.

Her advisor didn't take the time to really understand her better. She also asked her advisor to invest some of her money in "ethical funds," a basket or group of mutual fund stocks, where the money is invested in companies whose values align to her values. For example, funds that support clean energy or clean water production. Her advisor, who is female, dismissed this request. The woman was dumbfounded by the response to her request. Her advisor did not want to engage in conversations about these investments. No reason was given. Unfortunately, these two events compounded and trust was broken between the two. I encouraged this woman to find a new advisor because there clearly wasn't alignment, good communication or trust.

Don't have blind trust in your planner or advisor. You need to be engaged in the decision-making process, understand the investments in your account or portfolio, be consulted on how your money will be invested, take into consideration your risk profile, investment objectives and time horizon for needing the money.

Overall, lack of engagement with money can result in poor decisions or a total reliance on an advisor's decisions on how to manage our money, which may not be in alignment with our values or wishes. Even if we have someone managing our investments or money on our behalf, we must still understand the basics and check in from time to time,

Each of us has a "money mindset" that reflects in our attitude toward money. The goal is to have a healthy attitude toward money, to recognize the importance money plays in our life and to work through any negative attitudes we may have about our money.

My relationship to money is healthy. I have a positive mindset about money in general. I am naturally optimistic but need to watch this about myself. My over-optimism needs to be tempered with some healthy scepticism. I see money as a tool to live my life. It gives me comfort and buys me lifestyle. Here is a peek into my past money experiences and how my attitude evolved. As a teenager, I worked two jobs during the summer months to fund my university education. I worked while at school to ensure I had spending money. I graduated and soon after found an entry level job with a good company. I was twenty-two when I moved out of my parents' home and starting living an independent life.

My goals were clear and specific. I created a plan for myself. I wanted to advance my career, buy my first home and stop paying rent, and start saving for my retirement. I had multiple goals in my Life Plan to execute simultaneously. I knew relatively little about investing other than I had a savings account. I saw the success others were having around me and I wanted the same. I was happy for them and knew in my heart I could achieve the same success. I just really didn't know where to start. The funny thing is, the starting point for me was staring me right in the face. I didn't have to go much farther than my employer at that time.

I had time on my side. I understood the time value of money. I also learned the difference between risk and return. I was encouraged in my first job to take advantage of my employer's benefits or stock purchase program. I started small and began investing in my company. I paid myself first, meaning that when I got my pay every two weeks the money was already deducted for my stock purchase so I didn't miss it.

The company paid the commission fees for purchasing the shares. I took advantage of their DRIP (dividend reinvestment plan). Instead of taking cash for the dividends (profits) they paid every quarter, I reinvested the dividends and bought more shares. I bought shares at different times. Sometimes I bought shares when the price was going up. Sometimes I bought shares when the price was dropping. I averaged the price of my share purchases through a method called Dollar Cost Averaging. This tool offers the ability to buy shares when prices are at different levels, for example, at $20.00, $25.00, or $27.00 a share. My share balances grew. I continued for three years until the point where I had enough money to buy my first home. You can also achieve the same effect of dollar cost averaging if you invest a large chunk of money. So this should not hold anyone back who wants to catch up today.

I began investing during a good period when the markets were climbing. This is also referred to as a "bull market." I had not experienced a "bear market," where markets retract and decline. I experienced investing successes, stretched myself and maximized my contributions. I tasted success in small juicy morsels. This success built my confidence and increased my desire to invest more.

After three years of working for this company, I wanted to grow. I looked for opportunities within but none were readily available. I had no idea where I wanted to go but had the confidence to know I would find it. With my investing success under my belt, I wanted more.

I found a terrific program, the Canadian Securities course offered through the Canadian Securities Institute in Toronto, Canada. It is mandatory for people who become advisors or financial planners. I took it and it changed my life forever. I grew my knowledge and understanding of the money markets. I graduated successfully and realized that my destiny was the financial services industry. During that time, I found a mentor, my mom, to help me grow my investment and stock and bond portfolio. She encouraged me to invest in solid blue-chip companies that are generally strong companies with consistent financial performance.

Most of us can play catch up and engage in better financial behaviours. The strategies may be different depending on where you are in your life stage but feel confident that there are solutions.

COOKING WITH GAS

The expression "cooking with gas" may not be familiar to everyone. It means to cook at an accelerated pace. Each of us can cook our money with gas by accelerating our savings. The more money we have, the greater the potential to reach our goals sooner. Most goals have financial implications. Learning about money is important. Understanding the basic terms is critical. You can't bake in the kitchen or follow a recipe to successful completion unless you understand how to cook, what ingredients you need and how to use your tools. Money is no different. We must understand how money works. Make the terminology part of your money vocabulary. Check out the resources at the back of this book for some basic information on key financial terms.

YOU NEED DOUGH

There are so many slang names for money: dough, bread, clams, cheddar, lettuce, moula, cash etc. I never even heard of some of the names before I started writing this book. We bake bread with dough. For most of us, our dough has the ability to increase our purchasing power, live with more comfort and enjoy a better lifestyle. It means more personal freedom and the ability to choose or make choices defined by our own terms. For some, it just means power and status.

Famous psychologist, Abraham Maslow, author of *Motivation and Personality*, created a hierarchy of human needs that refers to the process of fulfilling life goals, dreams, and passions throughout our life stages. When we have limited financial resources, our dough is spent on life necessities: food, clothing and shelter. The more money we have available the greater potential or opportunity we have to reach and fulfill our goals and dreams. This is called self actualization.

How we spend our money in the short term could have long term implications on our ability to enjoy the sweetness of retirement. But who can really look that far ahead to see their future self when living a good life today is what matters? The biggest conundrum we face is our inability to see into the future and to know exactly how much money we will need in retirement. Much of this will have to do with lifestyle choices, where we live, and our health.

The problem with our decision-making process is that we often don't make the best choices for ourselves. Scientific research shows that we make irrational choices in our life and with our money. We may sell our investments because of fear of loss. We may buy our investments when the markets are at all time highs. We may spend based on our future earning potential only to find ourselves out of a job in three months.

Dine In or Take Out

Everyday living is expensive. The cost of living has risen dramatically over the past decades. Our money must stretch further because our purchasing power is being eroded by the high cost of living. Everything costs more. Most of us have no idea how we spend our money. It's cumbersome to track and life is hectic already. It seems like another burden to take on. Who wants to reconcile bills and accounts at night when we just want to download and relax by watching TV?

Buying fresh, organic produce is expensive. In fact, on average, Canadians spent $7,739 a year on food or $21.20 a day per household. This doesn't seem like much at all. But remember, this is an average amount.

Many of us are spending a lot of money eating in restaurants. Yes, spending time with friends socializing is a great life experience, but the cost of restaurant food adds up. The reality is most of us don't track how much money we spend on most things, let alone our groceries. Those of us who write a grocery list at least know we are buying what we need. Time would be well spent figuring out how much we spend on food. Here are some food expense figures Statistics Canada to give you an idea of what people are spending on average:

AVERAGE HOUSEHOLD FOOD EXPENDITURE, BY PROVINCE (CANADA)	2011	2012
	$	$
Food expenditures	7,795	7,739
Food purchased from stores	5,588	5,572
Bakery products	560	532
Cereal grains and cereal products	337	362
Fruit, fruit preparations and nuts	669	688
Vegetables and vegetable preparations	623	574
Dairy products and eggs	860	855
Meat	1,017	1,038
Processed meat	381	397
Fish and seafood	202	177
Non-alcoholic beverages and other food products	1,320	1,346
Food purchased from restaurants	2,207	2,167

Many new-found foodies will spend thousands of dollars stocking their kitchens with the latest and greatest tools. It's easy to get carried away in excitement and spend money on things we think we need but don't. In the kitchen, you require the basics: a paring knife, cast iron skillet, mixing bowls, food processor, spoons etc. These don't have to cost a lot of money. Of course, it's good to have a well-stocked kitchen including a variety of cooking utensils. But sometimes it's easy to overlook the essentials—those classic cooking tools. Without them, it would be difficult or even near-impossible to cook.

In the kitchen, as in the rest of life and how we handle our money, it's all about essentials and balance.

Put the Dishes in the Dishwasher

When dishes pile up in the kitchen and in the sink, you can't cook. Not putting dishes in the dishwasher after finishing a meal is a bad habit in the kitchen. Cleaning up in the kitchen is as important as preparation. So is not eating enough fruits, vegetables and dairy products. Many of us have bad habits that we find difficult to break. Some of our bad habits can be impulsive too. Many of us have a sweet tooth. We may snack on sweets or chips when we would be better off making a better snack choice or just waiting, in favour of a proper meal.

This is "temporal discounting," where we view small rewards available now, such as a new pair of shoes, as more desirable than a bigger payoff down the road, such as having more money for retirement. The term comes from leading researchers on Behavioural Finance. David H. Freedman wrote about the topic in a great article in *Scientific American* called "Time-Warping Temptations." Researchers agree that this type of behaviour is very prevalent in many bad habits such as overeating, overspending and drug abuse. The basics of "temporal discounting" were demonstrated in an experiment using student participants at The University of Pennsylvania. They were given two options. The first option was a gift certificate they could use immediately. The second option was a gift certificate that could only be used at a later date, but the amount was larger. Guess which one the students selected? They selected the one that had the immediate gratification or pay-off, much like my chocolate bar.

Beware of the Gingerbread House in the Forest

Cooking is generally a methodical and well thought out process that usually requires a set of essential tools. It is not an impulsive activity. Stopping for fast food may be an impulse activity. When you are hungry and smell something wonderful in the air, it can entice you to buy on impulse.

Impulse spending behaviour is related to the immediate availability of funds from any source—cash, credit, gift certificates—as long as the access is immediate. The experiment by the University of Pennsylvania demonstrates how dangerous credit cards, loans and lines of credit may be in terms of human preference for instant gratification. When faced with making life decisions that involve money, the term "instant gratification" is opposed to mindfulness. Money we waste on goods or services we can enjoy today robs us of financial resources we may need to fund our goals that probably will take time to accomplish.

Show Me the Money Honey

Money is the vehicle or tool used to buy comfort, and lifestyle. But at every income level there are ways to reach satisfaction. The mean household income in Canada is $76,000. Researchers believe that there is a satiation point of happiness based on household income at $75,000 U.S. It means that our level of happiness peaks when our income or household income reaches $75,000 U.S. If we make twice that amount of money, we may be able to buy a more luxurious house in a coveted neighborhood but we are no happier then someone making $75,000.

At first glance it may be hard to believe that there is a satiation point around income and happiness because doesn't more money mean more happiness? For fun, I took a quick poll with those around me who agreed that having a good life is possible at a household income of $75,000. Yet, other researchers now believe that income and happiness are directly correlated. In other words, the more money we make, the happier we are. And, if we spend our money wisely on life experiences instead of things, we will be happier. Who to believe? Perhaps there is a different way of evaluating our happiness.

In May, 2013, a research paper published in the *American Economic Review*, written by economists Betsey Stevenson and Justin Wolfers from the University of Michigan, disagrees with the findings of Deaton and Kahneman about what they named the 'satiation point' of $75,000 a year.

Stevenson and Wolfers concluded that satiation is roughly a straight line that does not diminish or increase as incomes rise. The overarching finding by these University of Michigan researchers—validated in both rich and poor countries—is that money does buy happiness and that more money leads to more happiness! In fact, these researchers write "We find no evidence of a significant break in either the happiness-income relationship, nor in the life satisfaction-income relationship, even as annual incomes go up to half a million dollars."

No one can agree on whether money can buy happiness but this shouldn't matter. It is up to each of us to understand what money means to us. Some of us believe that money buys happiness, others believe it doesn't. If your money is used to help you achieve the goals you set in your Life Plan, you will no doubt find greater joy in your life. I want you to really think about how you feel because this is what matters. Sometimes we get too caught up with what other people think and lose our ability to take a point of view that feels right for us.

Were You Born a Great Cook?

No one is born a great cook. It takes time, patience and perseverance to learn. But many of us have no interest in cooking. We may have no idea how to start, and may just abandon the idea because it seems too daunting. Fear, worry and uncertainty can create havoc in the kitchen. When I first started cooking in my early twenties, I honestly had no idea what I was doing. I never spent much time with my mother in the kitchen. My mother is a wonderful cook. Growing up, there was always a seat at my mom's table. She prepared many meals from scratch and I grew up on typical European meals such as goulash, wiener schnitzel and German style potato salad. My mother never really embraced North American cooking, probably because she couldn't read English cookbooks when she first came to Canada.

When I finally started my cooking journey it was with basic recipes from Mom. I would call her to help me through a recipe and from time to time we discussed new recipes and approaches to cooking. I started small and as I found greater success I tried more difficult recipes. I didn't know where to start so I just started somewhere. I started with the most important meal of the day, breakfast, and learned to make

French toast. Like many young women learning to cook, I took a "test and learn" approach in the kitchen. "No one is born a great cook, one learns by doing." says Julia Child. I tried not to beat myself up when things didn't go well. I had to learn to take the pressure off myself and enjoy the process and journey.

Fear is a common emotion in life and in the kitchen. I was surprised to learn that many people have an actual fear of cooking. The term mageirocophobia is used to describe someone who is afraid of cooking. Some people are socially anxious and fear cooking for a large group of people. Who hasn't been nervous or anxious when twenty guests are invited to dinner? There are some people who find it difficult to even cook up something very basic, like scrambled eggs. You may be surprised to learn that mageirocophobia is common. Researchers have found the fear is really about having something turn out poorly or a fear of failure.

The first time I cooked a meal for guests I made some major blunders. Most of my family was away travelling but two of my sisters were in town and I invited them over for Thanksgiving dinner. I spent days shopping to make sure that I had every ingredient to make the perfect turkey. I borrowed the finest linens from a friend. I set my table to perfection.

Everything pointed to my success. We sat down at the table to say Grace and begin our meal. The turkey was the centrepiece. I was so proud of myself. My husband began carving the turkey and to my surprise and dread, the turkey was under-cooked! My older sister, Aina, quickly took action and put the turkey back in the oven. We wrapped up all the side dishes in aluminum foil and put them in the oven too. Forty minutes later we ate a fully cooked and delicious turkey.

Every time I make a turkey, the conversation at the table always turns to my first turkey cooking experience. I must admit I still do get a bit anxious every time I cook a turkey, so what I do now is cook it in advance of dinner sitting. That way, I can manage the cooking without the pressure of guests around. Preparing ahead of time has become such an effective strategy for me. Planning ahead has become a way of life for me because it is like an insurance policy for cooking disasters.

Don't Be a Turkey

For some of us, thinking ahead makes us uncomfortable because it's hard to envision our future self. This may cause unnecessary anxiety and stress because it reminds us that we are getting older. Who isn't?

But to get our money working for us, it is essential that we start early and get the time value of money on our side. How we see ourselves today reflects our attitude about ourselves and our environment. How we see ourselves growing older, matters. If we see ourselves growing older gracefully, we will have a positive journey. We will be mentally prepared to deal with the issues of aging.

Fear is a natural emotion. The typical response to fear is freeze, flight or fight. It's okay to be afraid of things we don't understand or real threats in our lives, but sometimes we can create false fear about our money. Many of us don't openly talk about our fears and remain silent.

Many women don't even realize that fear is holding them back. Many women I speak to are afraid of the stock market. I realized that the fear they have is not about the stock market but about losing money. Many women think the stock market is this big complex machine that requires a forty page manual to understand. Investing can be complicated, but there is a way to manage this through education and choosing a good advisor.

Some of us know someone who has experienced a large financial loss through stocks and we are fearful of the same fate. We need to recognize the role fear plays in our life and to manage this fear as it relates to our money. Fear needs to be managed much like the fear I have about cooking a turkey. I have learned to manage it by changing my habits. Once a person gravitates toward fear-based decision making and fear-based influences, they have lost value and grounding and they have closed their minds to the possibility of other perspectives. You don't have to be ashamed of being afraid but don't let fear hold you back in life.

Food For Thought

How could you increase your comfort about your money?

_____

_____

How could you feel more confident about your money?

_____

_____

Do you feel you have a healthy relationship to money?

_____

_____

How does money bring joy to your life?

_____

_____

THE FOOD PROCESSOR: FINANCIAL PLANNING

"Once you have mastered a technique, you barely have to look at a recipe again."
—JULIA CHILD

Any tool that will accelerate the cooking process and decrease the time doing mundane activities in the kitchen is worth its weight in gold. Preparation is one of the most important steps in the kitchen because without the right ingredients readily available, a tried and true recipe and proper tools, cooking is difficult. Before the food processor, prepping for meals was much more time consuming. Everyone pitched in to help, slicing and dicing vegetables and prepping other ingredients. The food processor changed everything. It made cooking quicker and more pleasurable. All of us need a 'money processor' to accelerate our money for better financial outcomes, and the best processor is a financial plan.

Eighty-one percent of people who have a financial plan feel on track with their financial affairs, increase their ability to save money, feel more confident they can deal with life challenges that have financial implications, and have the ability to splurge and indulge on life's luxuries. It doesn't get any better than that, does it? Getting our money working for us is essential when we think about the cost of life goals.

The cost of your life goals may surprise you. It surprised me. In Citibank's Citi Blog's article, "Putting a Price Tag on Life's Financial Goals" by Jonathan Clements, the approximate cost of different life goals are listed, and may cost us $1,500,000 or more. This will depend on our lifestyle choices, whether we have children, the state of our health and where we live.

Cost of Life Goals

Retirement:	$750,000
Long term care:	$87,000
Assisted living:	$42,000
Raising a family (one child up to age 18):	$300,000
Home ownership:	$280,000
College & university (one child):	$71,000
	$1,500,000+

Home is an important ingredient in our Life Plan. I live in one of the most expensive and wonderful cities in the world. For fun, I grabbed a piece of paper and pen and wrote out the total cost of my life goals. The price tag reached close to **$2.1 million!** The average house price in Vancouver is close to **$900,000**. A single detached home is close to $1.8 million in my neighbourhood.

Have an Expert Chef Cook Your Dinner

There are many global organizations whose mandate is to educate investors about current and upcoming changes to the industry and to create greater transparency in investing. Getting advice in a complicated financial world is a non-negotiable. You can't start cooking without a cookbook or simple recipes to guide the process.

The Investment Funds Institute of Canada (IFIC) are committed to developing a better understanding of investment funds, new regulations, the value of a financial advisor and understanding risk.

They approached me as a member of the social media, financial and investment community, and asked that I share some high quality content with my followers on social media. I happily shared their tweets and posted to Facebook and LinkedIn. Many people think they can invest on their own and generate excellent investment returns. Some may, but most won't. There is value in having an advisor to help you invest your money. Here is an easy-to-read chart that shows the value of investment advice and how the longer you get advice the more your investments will grow. It doesn't get any simpler than this.

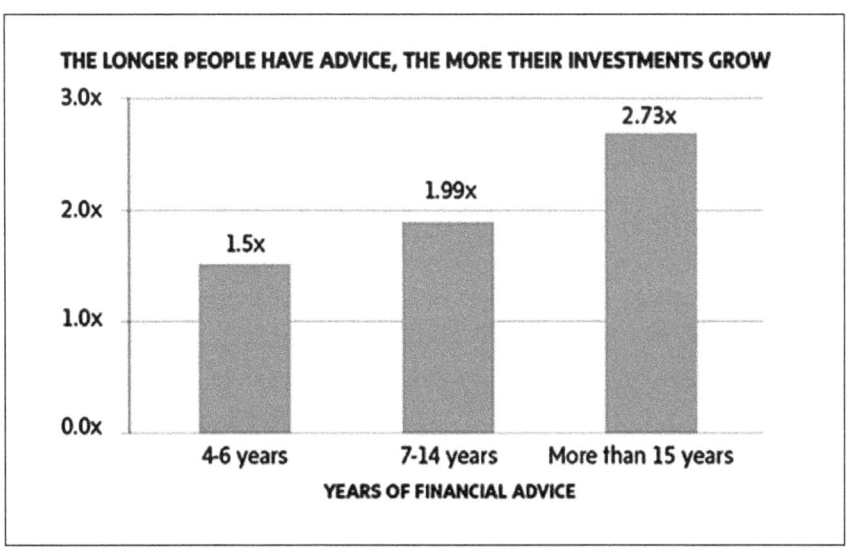

Ninety-five percent of wealthy women relinquish control of their money for investing because they feel they don't have the skills, knowledge or background to be successful. A leading American bank, State Street, released statistics in May, 2013, that indicated that women own 51.3% of wealth in the US—assets valued at more than eight trillion dollars. They believe it will increase to twenty-two trillion dollars by 2020. Over the next forty years, women are expected to inherit seventy percent of the forty-one trillion dollars in inter-generational wealth transfers. Increasing our financial capability matters more than ever!

Many organizations offer financial planning: financial institutions, credit unions, independent advisors, insurance companies, and more. Be very selective about the organization and individual you engage.

Advisors and financial planners offer financial planning. Financial planning is a great equalizer because every one of us has access to it. But only a small percentage of women have a financial plan. However, seventy percent of women who have a financial plan feel in control of their lives. Their emotional wellbeing skyrockets, they worry less about money and can focus on achieving their goals. A Life Plan and financial plan are the essential ingredients for living a delicious and nutritious financial life. Without them as a trusted partner to help guide you through the complex world of personal finance, you are at risk of making costly mistakes with your money and investments and may not reach your goals as quickly as you want. They offer a valuable service.

Advisors and financial planners offer a broad range of services to help us reach our goals. This includes investment planning, retirement planning, children's education planning, and major purchase planning such as a new home or vacation property.

They will spend time learning about our goals. They will not spend time fleshing out our goals or going through all the key considerations of goal-planning that you mapped out earlier. They will focus instead on creating an investment objective based on our goals. They will also consider our risk tolerance, and based on our age and financial situation, recommend investments that are right for us. They also take inflation and taxes into consideration when drawing up a financial plan.

A "full balance sheet" planner will look at our assets, investments, liabilities, loans and mortgages. This Big Picture is essential because our money has two sides to it. They will seek to elevate our financial position and are able to do so because they have a full picture of our money situation. They can also give us relevant advice on how to obtain a better credit rating or sustain a good one. They are experts and have deep and meaningful knowledge to share with us. A good planner or advisor will explain complex financial terms that you don't know or understand. You pay for this advice and knowledge but unless you are prepared to invest the time to become an expert, why would you even consider managing your investments or money on your own?

Once you get a financial plan it is important to follow through with it and not let it collect dust or hide in your filing cabinet. If you already have a financial plan, I would suggest that you make an appointment to update it. Your life goals may have changed, you may be going through a life transition or your financial situation may have altered. Stick to your financial plan and check in with your planner regularly.

There are three ways to get a financial plan:

1. **A financial plan prepared by an advisor or broker at your financial instition, insurance company or independant firm.** Financial planners and advisors in the banks, credit unions or caisse populaire will create a financial plan for you. It's free but they will sell you their own investments which could either be Mutual Funds or Exchange Traded Funds (ETFs). Sometimes there is a financial threshold (a minimum amount of money in your bank accounts) to working with someone in the branch. They will create a financial and investment plan that takes into consideration your investment objective, risk tolerance and invest your money.based on your risk tolerance.

2. **A fee-based financial plan prepared by an independant planner.** This person will create a financial plan and charge upwards of $2,000 for a comprehensive plan. They will work with an investment firm to invest your money. You don't have to work with this person. You can choose to invest your money with many different firms. For someone starting out or for someone who has yet to grow their savings, a fee-based financial planning will provide a much needed road map to get money growing.

3. **A financial plan prepared by you.** This is the DIY (do it yourself) approach to financial planning. There are many organizations that offer free financial planning software online. You can download the template and create a financial plan for yourself, partner or family. Here are a few websites that offer free software: http://mint.com or http://intuit.ca

Many people do prefer to work with a financial planner who is trained to create an individualized financial plan and has the skills, knowledge and background to help clients achieve life goals. One pot doesn't fit all, but if you have limited financial resources, a fee-based financial planner is likely the best. If you have acquired some savings and a good-sized nest egg, you may wish to engage a financial planner at your local bank or an investment advisor. These professionals will be able to help you achieve your goals and get your money.

Ingredients of a Financial Plan

Most financial plans are approximately ten pages long, connecting your life goals to your financial resources through sections on major purchase, education and retirement.

Here is an example of the type of information found in a comprehensive financial plan. Some areas may or may not be applicable to your situation today but may be applicable in the future.

Something Smells Fishy

Have you ever left something for so long in your fridge that when you take it out and open it the smell is so awful you gag? It can happen so easily but the smell will stink up your entire house for days. And fish seems to be one of the worst. When something smells fishy in our lives we are left feeling uncomfortable. Sometimes it can be the person. We can work with people who just don't feel trustworthy and dealings with them make us feel like something is off. It just doesn't smell right. Their actions and their words are incongruent. They don't answer

The 7 Segments of Life and Financial Planning

Life Planning
- What gets you up in the morning?
- For what are you striving in life?
- What excites you about your future plans?
- How do you see your personal or business legacy?
- What is important in your life today?

Cash Flow Management
- Sources, reliability and expected duration of current and future income
- Taxation of current and future income
- Expenses review and analysis
- Includes any Education funding requirements
- Income tax planning – personal, investment and business sources of income

Debt Management and Net Worth Enhancement
- Good Debt versus Bad Debt
- Analysis of Debt amounts, repayments, interest rates and purpose
- Restructuring opportunities for enhancing Net Worth growth
- Net Worth targets
- Non-retirement financial goals and objectives (education, asset acquisition, travel, etc.)
- Funding of goals from surplus or designated cash flow
- Includes all assets other than personal effects and non-realisable collectables, antiques and jewelry

Investment Management
- Individual Risk Tolerance Profiles
- Full investment analysis and review including purpose, goals and priority
- Targeted holdings and transition plans as appropriate
- Tax efficiency and effectiveness
- Includes business review from investment perspective including eventual disposition plans

Risk Management
- Lifestyle protection
- Asset protection
- Cash-flow protection
- Retirement protection

Estate Planning
- Legacy planning
- Survivor income and bequest planning
- Tax planning for your estate and legacy
- Charitable bequests (if applicable)
- Special needs bequests (if applicable)

Retirement Planning
- Current sources of income, duration, taxation and indexing
- Expected sources of income, duration, taxation and indexing
- Lifestyle objectives – 3 stages of retirement – lifetime income requirement
- Tax efficiency and effectiveness of income
- Protection of lifetime income from erosion by inflation

Courtesy of Ian R. Whiting, CD, CFP, CLU, CH.F.C., FLMI (FS), ACS, AIAA, AALU, TQFD-MF, LSSWB, Assoc. Member, Assoc. of Certified Fraud Examiners
E: ianw@customplanfinancial.com P: 604.888.3078 F: 604.888.3058

questions directly and we just don't feel good around them. It usually has to do with a deal or offer someone is pitching us.

No one likes someone double-dipping or sharing their glass with someone they don't know. There are germs to think about. You may be reluctant to relinquish control of your money and sceptical about trusting someone with it. Your friends and family may have not had a good experience. You have to be careful because there are people out there who will try to take advantage of you.

Get-rich-quick schemes have been around for millenia. Today we might refer to them as "Ponzi Schemes." Charles Ponzi was an Italian-born businessman and con artist operating in the U.S. and Canada in the 1920s. He promised clients a fifty percent profit within forty-five days or one hundred percent profit within ninety days. He took money he received from his first investors using money he received from later investors. His scheme ran for over a year before it collapsed, costing his 'investors' $20 million.

On one occasion, a well-meaning friend recommended I buy a speculative "penny stock" or low cap stock. I trusted this person. It was a highly speculative telecom stock and I didn't conduct the necessary due diligence (research) to really learn about the company and its potential. Thankfully, I only invested a small amount of money, but lost every penny (excuse the pun.) I had never experienced a financial loss to this point. Don't trust blindly even with well-meaning friends or family. This ultimately led to my investment philosophy, which is to "stick with what I know." And if I don't understand something, I need to take the time and effort to learn more before I part with my money.

Experts say that the 2008 financial crisis has eroded public confidence and trust in the United States government and financial system, however, the same was not found as much in Canada. Canadian banks are the exemplar of public confidence in banking. Trust is the most essential component of any relationship, especially in managing our money! Trust can take many forms, including trusting ourselves to make the optimal decisions for ourselves and our family. Trust also involves working with others and letting them manage our money. Diluted trust makes it harder to manage our money effectively.

For most women, it is hard to trust others with money. Managing our own money and that of our family is a major responsibility. We guard our money very closely because we know its power. It can help us get the life we want and it can take care of us as we grow older. Many women have stories of lost financial trust and the ensuing feelings of pain, anguish and remorse. All of us at some point have said, "How could I have been so dumb with my money?"

Commercial chefs trust their staff to make sure that meals are properly prepared and the kitchen is clean and safe. Trust is one of the hardest things to build and the easiest to lose. Building trust in someone when our financial future is at stake is a process that takes time. When engaging in conversations about our money, we are wise to enter the relationship slowly and gradually reveal personal and pertinent information. I share below, some tips on how to find an advisor we can trust. Referrals from friends are also a good way to find someone.

When we begin working with anyone new, particularly a financial services professional, there are three things they need to demonstrate: *credibility*, *reliability*, and *empathy*. The biggest challenge we will face is coming to terms with the fact that all financial advisors are in business to make money from us. Many people think their advisor is working for them, when in essence they are working for themselves. The trick is to find someone whose self-interest doesn't trump our needs.

Finding someone appropriate and trustworthy to work with can be a daunting task. You may not know where to start. If you are already working with people, ask yourself one simple question: "What have they done to show they value my business?"

Here are a few tips you might want to consider as you explore working with a new set of financial professionals:

Work with people you know. Rely on referrals from friends and family. Ask for references. People must earn your business so don't be afraid to interview several possible candidates before making your decision. Referrals are the greatest form of flattery and most people who get referred take referrals very seriously. Referrals result from doing a great job. Many businesses are built on referrals alone.

Seek expert advice. When dealing with a financial services organization, there are so many different layers and people working for them that it is hard to discern who to talk to. To find the right person, always double-check credentials to make sure you know who you are working with.

Know your needs. Make sure you are focused and that the other person knows what you need. Use the technique of *clarifying* and *confirming*. Clarify that the other person understands your needs and confirm this by having them repeat your needs back to you. This will ensure there are no misunderstandings. Make sure you have everything in writing; if you don't, there are no guarantees.

Expect empathy and understanding. Empathy and understanding builds trust and trust is what you need. When engaging in conversation about your money, it is imperative that the other person shows empathy and understanding. If they don't, then this is probably not the right person for you. I often hear from women that they prefer to work with other women simply because they require empathy in the relationship.

Expect an open and flowing conversation. Make sure your conversation is engaging and transparent and that there is a two-way dialogue. If someone is using industry jargon or terms you don't understand, ask them not to use the jargon and to explain things more clearly. Some financial professionals will try to wow you with their understanding of the market. You don't want to be wowed. Most women are looking for simple answers to complex questions.

Fully understand the terms and conditions. Read the fine print before signing anything. Remember, the devil's food cake is in the details. If you don't understand something, take time to reflect. Schedule another appointment. Never feel pressured.

Questions to Ask a Financial Planner

The Financial planning Standards Council in Ontario, Canada, a respected organization in North America, has developed a list of questions to ask prospective planners. I suggest you interview three prospective financial planners and ask them the same questions so you can compare their responses and find the most suitable candidate. Don't be afraid to ask other questions as well. Any professional will welcome them.

What are your qualifications?
Many people offering financial services call themselves financial planners. However, financial planning is a detailed, comprehensive process. It requires hands-on experience and a strong technical understanding of topics such as personal tax planning, insurance, investments, retirement planning, and estate planning. It requires understanding of how a recommendation in one area can affect other areas. Ask the planner what qualifications inform their financial advice. Ask what training they have successfully completed. Ask what steps they have taken to keep up with changes and developments in the financial planning field. Ask whether they hold any professional credentials, including Certified Financial Planner, which is recognized internationally as the mark of the competent, ethical, professional financial planner.

What experience do you have?
An important consideration in choosing any professional is their level of experience. Ask how long the planner has been in practice, the number and types of firms they worked with and how their work experience relates to their current practice. Inquire about what experience the planner has in dealing with clients in similar situations to yours and whether they have any specialized training. Choose a financial planner who has at least two years' experience in counselling individuals on their financial needs.

WHAT SERVICES DO YOU OFFER?

The services a financial planner offers will vary and depend on their credentials, registration, areas of expertise, and the organization for which they work. Some planners offer financial planning advice on a range of topics but do not sell financial products. Others may provide advice only in specific areas such as estate planning or taxation.

Those who sell financial products, such as insurance, stocks, bonds and mutual funds, or who give investment advice, must be registered with provincial regulatory authorities and may have specialized designations in these areas of expertise.

WHAT IS YOUR APPROACH TO FINANCIAL PLANNING?

Some planners prefer to develop detailed financial plans encompassing all the client's financial goals. Others choose to work in specific areas or services, as shown above. Ask whether the individual deals only with clients with specific net worth and income levels. Also ask whether the planner will help you implement the plan they develop or refer you to others.

WILL YOU BE THE ONLY PERSON WORKING WITH ME?

It is quite common for a financial planner to work with others in their organization to develop and implement financial planning recommendations. You may want to meet everyone who will be working with you. They often work with other professionals as well, including ones you already use, such as your lawyer and accountant.

HOW WILL I PAY FOR YOUR SERVICES?

Your planner should disclose in writing how they will be paid for the services provided. When planners are paid through commissions, they are compensated if you purchase financial products to implement a financial planning recommendation. In some cases, the commission is paid by the suppliers of financial products, such as an insurance company. In other cases, you pay the commission, for example, if you buy shares of a publicly traded company.

Food for Thought

It is wise to set up an interview with three planners or advisors and interview them. Now that you know what to expect, the process will be a lot easier. If you have a financial plan, you may want to touch base with your planner at least once a year because no doubt your life has changed and so have your goals. Reach out to your planner as soon as you can and share your goals.

Do you feel you have a better understanding of what is financial planning?

_____

_____

Do you understand the benefits of financial planning and what you could expect in a financial plan?

_____

_____

What, if anything, do you think would hold you back from getting a financial plan?

_____

_____

Future Dinner Parties

HUNGRY FOR MORE

"Just like becoming an expert in wine—you learn by drinking it, the best you can afford—you learn about great food by finding the best there is, whether simply or luxurious. Then you savor it, analyze it, and discuss it with your companions, and you compare it with other experiences."
—JULIA CHILD

Most of us are hungry for more. We can start looking ahead by planning our next get together and dinner party. Much like we plan ahead for major purchases, we want to have time on our side to prepare so we are not rushed. We have a new set of tools to use in our lives that will help us live with greater intent, find more meaning and joy. But the facts are clear, to find intent, greater meaning and joy in your life you must create a Life and Financial Plan.

We must grab hold of other kitchen helpers and tools we could use to help us achieve our goals in life and find more comfort from our money. Investing is a tool much like a paring knife that will allow us the ability to carve out our money and invest it across a broad range of investing tools. Investing is similar to aging wines and cheeses. There are wines that are meant to age and be consumed twenty or thirty years down the road. For example, we might be able to afford to buy a $100 of Chateaux Margot Bordeaux red wine today. A decade or two later, the bottle may be worth over $1,000. It is worth more because of the aging process. There are wines to consume today. Sommeliers or wine experts, carefully age wine. The wine must be stored at the right temperature and for the right amount of time. The fruits of investing generally appear down the road. Investing for a long life makes sense. A savings account is a starting point toward investing because it allows us the ability to accumulate money. But once we accumulate savings and wealth, what's next?

Barclays Wealth & Investment Management 2013 says, "Investors, as human beings, find it hard to balance what may be optimal long term decisions against different decisions that are made in the short term to reduce anxiety." The most important part of investing is managing our self and our behaviour.

Investing also includes real estate. Real estate investments as a primary residence is the single biggest investment we may make in our lifetime. This can be a good thing, but if we have borrowed a larger amount, stretching monies to be "cash poor" and becoming highly leveraged can adversely affect our lifestyle. Our real estate investments must fit into our life and financial plan.

Your Appetite for Learning

Become hungry for financial literacy. Let this hunger fuel your appetite for learning. Financial literacy is a must. My philosophy is really simple: I take a *just in time* approach to my knowledge base. There is a big BUT, though. We must have the fundamentals already in place about how money works. When I need more knowledge about financial issues, I follow this repeatable recipe:

First, I conduct my own research to become familiar with terms and concepts. Second, I engage professionals and get their advice and opinion. Third, I take time to reflect on the problem to be solved and the information available. I may run a few ideas by my family. I have the facts.

We can make decisions with imperfect information. We all do. We have to find confidence in the facts we have and know that any decision we make has been well researched and thought out.

Why I Love Aged Cheddar Cheese

One of my favourite things to do is to grab a wonderful bottle of French Bordeaux, a rich and deep red wine and pair it with a few crudités such as aged cheddar on a fresh baguette. The pairing is marvelous and pleases the palate. Aged cheddar cheese from France is a delight. It dances on your taste buds; a delicious and nutritious food that chef's love to work with.

Get time on your side and start aging your money today. Your future self will thank you. If we don't embrace our money today and increase our financial literacy, we risk paying for it later. Learning the basics about money is essential for today and the future. Make sure you understand at least the following terms and topics because they will help your money grow. Learn more about investing and personal finance at www.getsmarteraboutmoney.ca to get your money working for you. More definitions are at the end of this book.

- The time value of money

- How compounding interest works

- How the cost of living or inflation impacts the cost of food, clothing and shelter

- What are the real returns of our investments (commissions and fees)

- The difference between risk and return

- The different types of investments: stocks, bonds, ETFS, mutual funds, savings accounts

- The money markets where bonds, stocks, mutual funds and ETFs are traded

Budgets Are Like Grocery Lists

Keep track of how you spend your money. Budgets work. Plain and simple. Money needs a purpose and intent. In our lives, the purpose is our goals. Our money takes on a new intent when it is directed to something specific. For example, you will think twice about buying a new pair of shoes if one of your goals is to save more money to buy a house. You will want to redirect that 'extra' money towards your goal. You may also have to make some lifestyle changes.

For many of us, the "money in/money out" cycle is common. Wealthy women can be faced with this situation too. The money comes into our hands or our accounts as quickly as it goes out to meet our monthly expenditures. But most of our expenditures are driven by our lifestyle choices. With incomes that are not growing, our money is being squeezed. The cost of living is rising and if our money isn't growing we have to make trade-offs. Most of us are not prepared to give up our lifestyle. Something has to give.

The Pantry is Full

Throughout history, "pantry loading" has been done by women to stock up on canned foods in the event of emergencies. Today, pantry loading offers a cost effective way to stock up on expensive staples when they go on sale.

Each of us will have a different financial situation. Some of us may be carrying record debt. We may have more debt, but many of us are worth more. Does that make it alright to carry high levels of debt? I don't think so. For many of us, our homes have significantly appreciated in value. The stock market has recovered from the 2008 financial crisis. But many of us owe more then we have in disposable income. We waste money on impulsive purchases instead of redirecting it towards debt, savings or other priorities. It's the same as pouring something down the drain. On average, people spend approximately $3,500 on impulse buys a year that they regret. Fifty percent return their purchases.

Some of us may be born savers or spenders. I am a spender and have to be really careful not to spend money mindlessly. By mindlessly I mean taking out my wallet or using my credit card with little thought or awareness of what I am actually doing. When this happens, I am usually distracted in thought, talking to someone else or not being fully present in what I am doing. According to Rick Scott, Cynthia Cryder and George Loewenstein in their article on "Tightwads and Spendthrifts" in the *Journal of Consumer Research 34*, there are two types of money personalities, a "spendthrift" or a "tightwad." We may sometimes find ourselves in between but most of us have a tendency either way.

Spendthrifts find it easy to spend money because they tend to feel relatively little pain when doing so. A tightwad holds on to their money and it is possible to observe their pain as they hand it over in payment for something. This pain threshold makes it extremely difficult for tightwads to overspend or indulge themselves.

Let me introduce you to Sarah, seated at our table. She is a spendthrift. I share this story to demonstrate how spending can easily get out of control and tempt financial ruin.

The following story was sent to me by Linda Chu, a professional organizer based in Vancouver, who is the founder of *Out of Chaos: Professional Organizing Solutions*.

Sarah's parents had lived in their home for over fifty years. Like most parents of their generation, "waste not, want not" was the motto. Sarah moved back into her parents' home after her mother's passing. Her father had died years before. Since Sarah was single and had no children, the house was too big for her to manage on her own. She wanted to sell since it would fetch a good price. Her intention was to clean out the rooms full of personal possessions and a lifetime of collections so that she could put the house up for sale. That intention is now five years old.

Since her mother passed, Sarah found herself immersed in the memory of each object. Her intention of clearing became an emotional battle between living in the past and wanting to sell. Living in the past is like having a fridge full of leftovers. We eat them because we don't want to waste but we would rather have fresh items to nourish us. Sarah became consumed by guilt about letting go of items that meant something to her parents. Try as she would, it was almost impossible to clear away anything, not even items that had no value to her. Compounding the situation was everything that Sarah had collected in the five years since taking over the home. Her collection of magazine subscriptions, cooking journals, and other things created clutter.

Consider the financial cost to Sarah over the five years. If she had sold the house five years earlier and invested the money, what would be the value? If we add up all the magazine subscriptions and incidental magazine purchases she had made over five years, how much money had she spent on unread materials?

Sadly, it was her own health crisis that led Sarah to reach out to enlist the help of the professional organizing company run by Linda Chu. Sarah finally accepted that she needed help. She realized that despite the emotional attachment to her parents' home, she did not have the physical capacity or the financial means to maintain such a large home, especially once she started to consider her dream of taking a trip every year.

Stirring Up the Pot

Food and money have many things in common. It's important to have a healthy relationship with food. Some of us have an emotional relationship with it while others have a more physical relationship. We eat when we are hungry. In order to have a healthy lifestyle, it is important to have a healthy diet and eat nutritious food. Food can have power over us emotionally. Many of us know of someone who is an emotional eater. Some people turn to food when they are stressed out, had a fight with their partner or a difficult day at work. Food can offer comfort. Food can temporarily fill an empty stomach but never fill an empty heart. What we stock in our kitchens and life, matters.

Cooking is an emotional experience. Whether it goes well or goes poorly, there is so much emotion in the kitchen. A negative mood is a precursor to spending money. This is emotional shopping. A negative mood is a precursor to emotional eating. Emotional shopping differs from compulsive shopping. Emotional shopping can be compulsive when it occurs repeatedly, but it can also be occasional. All of us have engaged in emotional shopping where we spent money to feel better. We shop to fill a void. Repeated cycles of emotional shopping can lead to huge bills and debts that can be difficult to control. Emotional shopping is one of the biggest challenges many of us have when it comes to managing money.

We must evaluate the daily emotions we have that might trigger bad money habits such as overspending. When we are feeling emotional, do we find ourselves geared up and ready to spend money? When we have had an argument or a stressful interaction with someone in our daily life, do we spend more?

"Living large" is spending money to the extreme, with little thought to the long term consequences or outcomes. Many of us know people who are doing just that. Their credit card bills and lines of credit are maxed. Yet, how could they stop when they are in the vicious cycle of living large: big mortgage, extended line of credit and holding crippling debt while working a job they hate. They can't afford to quit. Some of us may find ourselves in dead-end jobs that drive these behaviours. Everyday living is probably not very satisfactory and if you see yourself at all in this description please make sure your new goals address your unhappiness.

Fast Foods and Convenience Cards

Convenience foods help busy women. They may cost more money to buy but lift the burden off women and provide much needed help. Credit cards offer convenience too. You can travel almost anywhere in this world and be able to pay for food, hotels and other travel related expenses with ease and little concern. Credit cards are one of my favourite payment methods. They only become an expensive tool when balances are not paid in full, otherwise the convenience they offer is unmatched.

Credit cards can offer many really good benefits including the collection of points to be used for future travel etc. Some offer free groceries, travel miles and other attractive bonuses. I have met many people who use their credit cards to pay for everything they purchase. The added benefit is it makes monthly household budgeting and record-keeping easier.

Over-Indulging at the Buffet

Over-spending is much like over-indulging at the local buffet. It happens. Who hasn't over-indulged in life a few times with credit cards and run a balance? We don't even realize we are doing it. If we over indulge, spend on our credit card and can't pay off the balance, something has to give. We pay hefty fees and interest that eats away our finances. It's like a bottomless pit! When we find ourselves with too much debt or balances on our credit cards we must take action. Paying $200 to $300 dollars in interest every month on a credit card is crazy silly. It's like having a stomach ache after eating too much.

If debt is eating you up, here is a way to shed a few pounds.

Stop spending. The easiest way to stop doing something that isn't good for us is to just stop and say "No" to the impulse. Each of us can choose differently.

Keep track of credit card spending. Save receipts and check them against your monthly statement. If you have a hard time resisting a good deal, leave your card at home or put it into a safety deposit box.

Carry only one credit card. Most of us carry at least three or more credit cards in our wallets. All of them no doubt carry fees and it's hard to remember which one we used last or why we even have so many cards. The only time you need to have two cards in your wallet is if you travel on business or on vacation. You never want to find yourself in a foreign country and learn that your credit card has been declined.

Consolidate credit card balances. If we find ourselves carrying balances on our multiple credit cards, consolidate the balances and get a loan at a lower interest rate to pay off the balance. Add up how much you are spending on interest every year. You may be shocked.

Plan ahead. The best way to make a major purchase down the road is to start saving money today. Business uses a tool called "accruing." It means to begin saving money now for future purchases down the road. They may save money during a good period in their business. This way they set aside money for things the business will need down the road. We must accrue for things we want to buy.

A friend of mine loves to plan ahead for her vacations. Three to six months before she goes on vacation she starts a saving strategy where she tosses loose change into a jar. It's simple. In most cases, she saves enough money to pay for her incidental costs while she is away. She never misses the loose change and the added benefit is her wallet is less cluttered. If you can't keep your hands out of the cookie jar, convert the change into bank drafts periodically, which will make you think twice about spending your vacation cash before you are on vacation. Many of us will use credit to pay for a vacation and start paying off the credit card balance when the bill comes in. For example, a $1,200 vacation is no longer a bargain or good deal if it really costs $3,000 with interest. None of us would brag to our friends about this.

Over-Cooked Dinner

A four-ribbed prime rib roast au jus with a hint of rosemary, buttery cooked carrots with a dash of basil, and mashed potatoes is one of my favourite meals to prepare for Sunday dinner. The best way to cook it is slowly, to ensure the juices remain in the meat. If it is cooked correctly, the meat melts in your mouth. If it is over-cooked, the meat will be chewy and disappointing. Because prime rib is expensive, it requires extra care to make sure the meat remains tender. I once overcooked a prime rib because I was distracted doing something else. I felt horrible when I served it for Sunday dinner. I vowed never to make that mistake again.

We can make mindless decisions with our money when we don't take the time to really understand our thoughts, feelings and actions around our choices. Without realizing it, our emotions can have a profound influence on our actions. It doesn't matter how much money we have or make—all of us are vulnerable to engaging in mindless behaviour.

The idea of being fully present and very aware of our surroundings is called "mindfulness." It supports the idea that when we are more mindful or present we are more receptive and open and non-judgmental. It's easy to see how mindfulness plays out in the kitchen. Many of us feel distracted in our lives. Distraction in the kitchen can lead to problems, including injury. But the kitchen offers us the ability to relax and become really present in what we are doing. We smell, taste, touch and feel our food. We take our time to prepare recipes and become very present or even in touch with the foods we are handling and preparing. We are fully engaged in the process, have fun and enjoy the culinary experience.

You may be surprised to learn that leading North American businesses have embraced mindfulness and meditation. They are seeing the benefits of this new path in greater productivity as a result of their employees becoming more centered, calm and aware, and make better and more informed life-work balance choices.

Target, Google, Twitter, Facebook, General Mills and Sun Life Financial are just some of the organizations that have embraced helping their employees become more mindful. Mindfulness training has also helped organizations retain employees who are best suited to the company's culture and values. Through greater insight and choice, we can transform our self and how we engage in any activity.

The Buddha said that a person should establish mindfulness in one's day-to-day life maintaining, as much as possible, a calm awareness of one's body, feelings, and mind. Mindfulness is an attentive awareness of the reality of things (especially of the present moment) and is an antidote to delusion about our circumstances. Mindfulness becomes a power when it works with a clear understanding of what is taking place, and can be traced back to ancient Hindu scripture.

Practitioners of meditation report increased awareness, focus and concentration as well as a more positive outlook on life. Although there are many different approaches to meditation, the fundamental principles remain the same. The most important principles are those of removing obstructive, negative and wandering thoughts and calming the mind with a deep sense of focus. This clears the mind of debris and prepares it for a higher quality of activity.

Negative thoughts can be redirected through the practice of mindful meditation. Shutting these thoughts out allows for the cleansing of the mind so that it may focus on deeper, more meaningful messages from the soul. Some practitioners even shut out all sensory input—no sights, no sounds, and nothing to touch—and try to detach themselves from the commotion around them. We may focus on a deep, profound thought if this is our goal. It may seem uncomfortable at first, since we are all too accustomed to constantly hearing and seeing things. But as we practice, we can become more aware of everything around us with greater clarity.

We can use meal time and the eating of food as an experience to encourage mindfulness. This can be done by eating more slowly and paying attention to the texture, taste and form of our food. It's relaxing. Meal time should be a relaxing and enjoyable experience, and not something that is rushed or indigestion will occur. When you gather for meals with friends and family, take your time, not only to enjoy the company by being very present and in the moment, but to enjoy your food too, every last morsel. There is gratitude. When we buy fast food on impulse or the chocolate bar at the grocery store or gulp down our food on the run, we engage in mindless and impulsive behaviour. There is little value.

When we engage in conscious choice we are mindful of our actions. We are self-aware. When we make mindful money decisions we spend our money with intent and clear direction. We don't squander or waste it. We may make trade-offs but we are conscious how we trade off one thing for another. For example, we may struggle to know what to do with our money and may have competing priorities: buying a new car, saving for our kid's education or renovating the kitchen. It's difficult to make a trade-off between all three. That's where financial planning comes in because the process can help us perhaps achieve all three! There is nothing more empowering than being in control of our money instead of letting it control us. When we engage in mindful spending we are in control of our lives. It empowers us to make good choices. Mindfulness creates peace of mind and feelings of gratitude.

Nobody Likes Leftovers

In the kitchen, food waste is organic and we compost what we don't need. Reduce. Reuse. Recyle. Living frugally is one approach some people take. They are minimalist in how they live. They buy what they need. They don't waste food or money on things that are of zero value. They are not "cheap." People who are "cheap" tend to only buy low quality goods because of the price point. They will trade off value for price. Low price can often mean low quality. Buying on sale is different.

There is currently a global trend towards less conspicuous consumption and the rise of thrift. People are becoming more mindful about waste and clutter. To that end, material items are being repurposed at little cost. The term "liquid life" has been used to refer to extending the life of an object. For example, bikes, toys and books may be sold or given away several times over.

In addition, the "barter economy" is growing, in which many of us are exchanging goods and services with each other with no exchange of money. For example, someone may be a hairstylist and provide their services in exchange for babysitting services. At our old stone cottage, we are forever bartering something for something else. It is almost expected and it's quite fun.

These global shifts in consumer behaviour are creating a new economy, the "Cinderella Economy," where many of us are "renting lifestyle":

getaway places, homes, cars, boats etc., for a short period of time instead of purchasing them and going further into debt. This trend may eventually replace the need to keep up with the Joneses. Thank goodness!

Even with these shifts, we still live in a consumption-based culture. In the last half century our society has moved from a saving culture to a spending culture. The earliest part of this cultural swing might have begun before WWI but it definitely took hold during the Roaring Twenties. It stalled during the Great Depression of the 1930s but spending became popular again after WWII and accelerated rapidly during the 1950s, when it was within reach for most working and middle-class households to have a "car in every driveway" and every modern electrical appliance.

When the first of the Boomer generation became adults in the early 1960s, there was nothing stopping them. They were off to the races! During the 1970s nobody paid much attention to the oil crisis and other drastic warnings. By the end of the 1980s conspicuous consumption was totally obscene, and has been going full tilt ever since, for those who can afford it or not.

Traditionally, some marketing involves trickery. False promises are made to consumers, such as getting rich quickly, looking younger, and getting thinner. Many organizations that try to entice us to spend our money are playing on our weaknesses and vulnerabilities.

It is easy to be persuaded to buy something when we are feeling emotionally drained or stressed. It is harder to be influenced or tricked when we are in top form. Yet, even for those who are very self-aware and mindful, the subconscious can be programmed by watching television, listening to radio, looking at billboards and watching advertising go by on buses.

Recipes From Around the World

There are as many different ways to improve our financial standing as there are foods in this world. Not only have we become global citizens and can easily travel from one country to another, our palate or choice in food has broadened. Many of us grew up eating meat and potatoes. Many of us are turning to vegan and prefer not to eat meat. That is perfectly acceptable to have an eclectic and diverse palate. Today, we eat fusion food, blended cuisine, for example, Tex-Mex. We are consuming authentic ethnic foods including Asian, South Asian, Thai, Malaysian, Mexican, and Mediterranean. Feast your eyes on a curry stew or chicken enchilada. Rice, nacho chips and salsa are part of our daily diets. Sushi is no longer a delicacy, its mainstream.

I love to borrow my friends' recipes and try them. Sometimes I find success, sometimes I don't, but I learn something new in the kitchen every day. I get inspiration from other chefs. My mother inspires me to be the best I can be. I am inspired by women who have overcome adversity in life and rebounded to find greater success.

For example, Audrey Hepburn inspires me because she lived a value-centred life, a global icon that lived a life of grace and style. She took some major risks in her career and the parts she played in movies. She was known for taking long walks with her Yorkie, Mr. Famous. After she married, she still made it a point to engage in 'me time.' She kept a house in Switzerland for quiet retreats. "I have to be alone very often. I'd be quite happy if I spent from Saturday night until Monday morning alone in my apartment. That's how I refuel." She believed in thoughtful reflection. She engaged in hobbies. She found her own sense of style.

Confidence in life comes from knowing where we are going and having mini-successes along the way. It also comes from testing new approaches or doing things we have never done before. Many of us want to be bigger, but in order to figure out what bigger is we need to tap into our minds and hearts to see where that leads us.

Age Wine Gracefully

There is wine to consume today, and wine to consume tomorrow. Buying wine can pose a dilemma for us because we have to make a decision whether to buy a wine to consume today or tomorrow. The latter will need to age in a wine cellar, pantry or cupboard. It is to be enjoyed at much later date, perhaps ten to twenty years later. We delay gratification in drinking this wine because it will taste better. But the aging of wine improves its quality only if the wine was designed to be aged. Wine is perishable and you won't enjoy it if you try to age it when it was never meant to age. Many of us have grabbed a bottle from our wine collection only to find it has not aged well (because it was never meant to age) and tastes more like vinegar. It's disappointing. Much like our lives, there are goals we want to achieve today or soon and there are goals that are longer term.

A wine cellar needs a vision. It isn't something you can just whip up. It requires thoughtful planning. The wine's structure or make-up will determine how well it ages. There are many elements to wine: acidity, sugar, tannins. There can be a bit of guess work to figuring out which wines is age worthy and sometimes even the experts get it wrong.

Our goals are like fine wine. They generally fall into two categories: short and long terms. A short-term goal is something we want to accomplish in no longer than six month s. For example, a short term goal might be to lose ten pounds, or take a vacation. Or the goal could be long term, over five years, like saving for retirement. Again, this will need a disciplined approach to saving money.

Slow Cooking

Many women I know love the slow cooker. They are making a big come back. They used to be called crock pots. The slow cooker is not at all like the pressure cooker. It helps cook a balanced meal all in one pot in just a few hours, reducing preparation time and freeing us up to do other things. Slow cookers are so easy to use. It takes only a few minutes to set up once you have the right ingredients and recipe to follow. You can take the least expensive ingredients from the grocery store and create a culinary delight. All you need to do is fill it up and put it on low and cook for a very long time. Sometimes the best food is the simplest in ingredients and preparation.

Life is one big slow cooker. Every woman needs a slow cooker approach to her life to help simplify and streamline. It mustn't be rushed or we will miss it and we need to plan for a very long cooking time. We must balance our needs for today with our needs for tomorrow. Here are some things to keep in mind about slow cooking your life:

🍽 Plan for a long life

🍽 Live by your Life Plan

🍽 Live by your Financial Plan

🍽 Regularly update your Life and Financial Plan

🍽 Invest your money in the stock and bond markets

🍽 Spend money mindfully

Get time on your side. The sooner we start, the sooner we find success. Don't wait. Time can be one of our worst enemies the older we get because if we make a mistake we may not have much time to recover. Stay committed. It is so easy to abandon something when the results are not forthcoming immediately. We live in an instant gratification world and want results now, not later. It is easy to get side-tracked by short term needs and forget about the needs of tomorrow. The average life expectancy for women is eighty-four in Canada and getting longer.

We may take one look at our savings account, and say forget it, there is no way we will ever have enough dough. For most of us, the only way we are ever going to be able to afford to achieve all our goals is to take

$1.00 today and turn it into **$5.00 tomorrow**. To follow is an example of how to grow our money and leverage the time value of money.

If we are in our twenties we probably want to accomplish many things and some may require financial resources. This is the optimal part of our lives to get time on our side and commit to an investment/savings strategy. The "*set it and forget it*" approach. It's a popular term used to describe the idea of putting something in motion and letting it take its course. If we start saving now we can forget about worrying. How empowering is that? For example, if we have $5,000 saved and over the next thirty years add $100 per month with an interest rate of 4.5%, our savings would be worth $95,177.10. This is the time value of money. To see for ourselves, try the savings calculator at www.bankrate.com.

Most of us could easily find $100 a month to save. For example, we could bag our lunch and make coffee at home. Don't boil the ocean. Make small incremental changes to spending. If we can afford to save more than $100 a month, do so. Our future self will thank us. This is slow cooking. We need our money to simmer for a very long, long time.

If we are in our thirties, forties or fifties, we probably have a different set of priorities as we saw at the beginning of this book. We are most definitely focused on our career and work. We may have a set of new goals we want to accomplish. Living the best life today, matters. We can outsmart longevity risk by starting monthly contributions or increasing our monthly contributions to accelerate growth of our retirement nest egg. Some refer to this as "catch-up."

However, the only difference with being older and being in our twenties is that our time horizon is shorter and we will have to accelerate our savings to compensate. Taking the above example, we will need to add more money and lessen the time horizon. If we have saved $5,000 and save $250.00 a month for the next twenty years with an interest rate of 4.50% compounded, our final savings is $109,308.42.

Maximize your contributions. Sun Life Financial Inc. found that men are contributing more to their employer sponsored savings plan than women. The average annual contribution in 2013 by men was $5,610 where females only contributed $3,775. Women must maximize employer matching in their plans.

Icing on the Cake

Take advantage of **all** your employer benefits. Some of us may feel we are working for peanuts, but you may be surprised that your benefits can account for approximately thirty percent of your compensation package if you use all of them. Your employer may help fund your retirement, go back to school or get braces for your kids. It takes a lot of after-tax dollars to pay for these life necessities. Read the fine print and find the hidden money. Many of us have wonderful employee benefits that we are not using and could help us to save more money to reach our goals or plan for our retirement. Benefits may include education assistance, stock purchase programs and retirement savings. There could be other benefits offered, such as special pricing on computers or other items, childcare support and standard benefits such as medical and dental coverage. There may be tax implications to the benefits, but nine times out of ten the benefit will far outweigh the tax burden.

And finally, most benefit plans allow employees to make changes once a year or at the time of a major life event. This is important because we might not have to wait until the annual review process to make these changes. Many people don't sign up because they think they will not be with their employer long and the paper work is cumbersome.

Even if you plan on staying only a few years, enroll. You won't regret it. This is "free" money and "free" is always best. Talk about icing on the cake!

Take a long term view of your life and financial plan and check in regularly to make sure you are on track. You may have to make adjustments particularly if a life event occurs that gets you off track for the short term.

Be mindful of how you spend your money. Avoid impulse purchases that may feel great now, but you may regret them later. Clutter can accumulate and eventually it will end up in the garbage. You are throwing your hard-earned money away. Save and spend your money on goal-related pursuits or life experiences. Use your credit card for convenience only and pay off your balances every month. Credit-card interest is close to twenty percent.

Spend Your Money in the Kitchen

Elizabeth Dunn, the author of *Happy Money, The Science of Smarter Spending*, is an inspiration to me in daily life, and I refer to her expert research as I go about my work. Dunn offers her research as a foundation for the importance of spending money wisely in order to increase happiness. She debunks many cultural myths about what makes us happy. I encourage everyone to read her book. She points out the importance of spending money on life experiences and explains that spending on others is a sure-fire way to derive more satisfaction from our money.

Don't Cry Over Spilled Milk

Unfortunately, you can't plan and orchestrate everything because a life event could change it all. There are over ninety identified life events we could experience. To learn more about what they are, please send me a note at anita@anitasaulite.com. Some of them will be planned and others may be unexpected. Each of us responds differently to change. When a tragic life event happens and sets you back, the strategy is not to cry over spilled milk but to work through the transition. You clean it up and move forward. Here are ten life transitions to consider:

🍴 Suddenly single

🍴 A sudden change in your financial situation

🍴 Loss of employment income

🍴 A new job

🍴 A change in your health

🍴 Leaving home for the first time or returning home

🍴 Getting a divorce or separation

🍴 Moving to a new city

🍴 An unexpected inheritance or windfall of money

You may be experiencing at least one or two of them right now. How you manage them will determine your movement forward.

Life transitions will set your life and money in motion and may result in a loss or gain. Losses are the most difficult to work through but gains can also be challenging. You will come through these events intact if you control your life by taking specific steps to get yourself back on track. Make no mistake; a life transition or event can detour you off your path.

An unexpected event can change everything. Job loss, death of a loved one, sudden loss of money, divorce, a new health concern, can have life-long emotional and financial impacts. Life events will happen, so you will need a Go-To plan to successfully navigate through a life transition.

Frugal is In, Cheap is Out

There is a big trend going on right now. It's called being frugal. Being frugal is not about being cheap at all. It's about being more mindful with our money and choosing to spend it on quality food and not waste. Most of us have a clear picture of someone who has "made it"—someone who is a millionaire. But we might be surprised to learn how they really live, what they value, and how they spend their money.

You may think they buy a new car every year, live in a fancy house and spend money like crazy. You may also think they are the head of a major corporation in North America and are on the top of the Fortune 500 list. Let's take a quick peak to see who some of them are.

Thomas Stanley and William Danko's book. *The Millionaire Next Door* revealed that most millionaires really could be the folks next door. They don't buy a new car every year or fly around the world in private jets. In fact, sometimes they're the least likely person we would suspect. This is what they do:

- Live below their means

- Live a frugal lifestyle

- Are self employed

- Plan and study investments

- Are self-made. They didn't inherit sums of money or grew up in a wealthy household.

They exhibit excellent qualities about how to manage money, spending and living within their means. They are very engaged in their investing. They don't give in to impulsive shopping but don't regret purchases either. They are tightwads with their money and hang on to it.

Start a Dinner Party Log

Foodies like me keep track of our dinner parties in a diary. It's an important tool to have particularly if we host a lot of dinner parties—what was served, who attended etc. We do this in order to celebrate our successful events, to keep track of what went well and what didn't go well. The log is a useful tool because it helps with scheduling more parties. Sometimes it is hard to remember all of the details in our busy lives.

Most of us have To-Do lists where we keep track of things we need to accomplish on a weekly basis. There is so much satisfaction that comes from ticking the box or scratching an item off the list. But many of have long lists. We feel we can never accomplish much because as soon as we tick the box there is more to add to the list. This stresses us. We need to counter-balance our To-Do List with an Accomplishment List. Why?

Most of want to win in life and keeping tally of things we accomplish acts as a silent partner to help us accomplish more. We feel good about ourselves and this propels us forward. We don't have to accomplish a goal fully to feel success. For example, if your goal is to lose twenty pounds and you have lost four pounds already, this is a quick win, an important step towards a bigger goal. It's worth stopping the cooking timer to celebrate. For example, if your goal is to go to Paris and last time you checked you saved $800 towards the trip, celebrate this mini-success. You are 25% closer to reaching your goal. And when you get to Paris, well . . .

Mini-successes or steps along the way to a big goal are important reminders that we are progressing.

Thanks For Joining Me Around the Table

MI CASA ES SU CASA

"The more you know, the more you can create. There's no end to imagination in the kitchen."

—JULIA CHILD

As we wind down the evening, our time together is coming to an end. It has truly been a joy to celebrate and share our life stories. Following the traditions of our mothers, grandmothers, great grandmothers and other women before us is the finest way to honour our past and look to our future. My house is your house.

The culinary world can teach us much about our lives. Food gives us comfort much like our money. None of us wants to work for peanuts. We can't enjoy a half-baked life. And aged cheddar cheese and vintage wine resemble fruits of our labour. A cast iron skillet, like our money, is a tool to help us live. It is essential and we must take care of it. All of us want to cook with gas, and when you take a Life Plan and pair it with a Financial Plan, the food processor in our lives, you have the power to create a culinary delight that is rich, full of nutrients and has staying power for a lifetime.

The best food is the simplest to make. You can't rush the cooking process. All of us begin with a heat-up that turns into a boil, and cools down to a simmer. Just like the stages of our life.

Success tastes good. Its colour and the flavour delights. It comes in all shapes and sizes, and for most of us, it comes in bite-sized appetizers or a two-bite brownie®. Most of us will never cook a show-stopping masterpiece because we leave that for the culinary chefs in this world. We spend every day cooking meals that have intent and create meaning. We find joy in this simple life pleasure.

We crave authenticity in our food and with people. We must give value to everything in our lives. The value today. The value tomorrow. The value of a life well lived and the value of our money. Both matter. Planning for a long, delicious and nutritious life is the ONLY strategy you need.

Live a joyful life. Be grateful. Take time to prepare a gratitude list of the riches in your everyday life, the relationships that matter and your health.

Stop your cooking timer once in a while to be more aware and mindful of how you live every day and the choices you make today. Learn to love the slow cooker.

Our minds get hungry for ideas. I hope yours is full.

Kitchen Utensils And Supplies

ESSENTIAL INGREDIENTS

Asset allocation: This is a process whereby someone spreads their money across a broad range of asset classes in order to reduce risk. For example, we could have an asset allocation of 40% in stocks, 40% in bonds, and 20% in cash. Asset allocation is typically used to reduce risk and exposure to the market. For someone who is risk adverse, they may have more money in cash or bonds. For those who are higher risk tolerant, assets could be as high as 60% in stocks. Much of this depends on age, time to retirement, need for funds, and risk tolerance. If a person cannot afford to lose any money, their risk tolerance would be lower. Many women have lower risk tolerance than men. This is a proven fact and we need to be mindful of this in our conversations about investing.

Bear market: A bear market is opposite to a bull market. This is when a group of stocks or securities are expected to decline. Often many of us will say they are "bearish about a stock," meaning they expect it to drop or fall. Or someone may say they are bearish about the market, which means they anticipate the entire market dropping or falling.

Bonds: A bond is a debt instrument or investment. It is a certificate that a company or the government can issue, promising to pay the holder a specific amount of interest for a specific length of time, and to repay the loan on maturity. Assets are generally pledged as security for a bond issue. Bonds trade like stocks. They pay interest at set amounts on regular or specific dates. Companies will issue bonds and sell them to the public, because in some countries it is a cheaper way for a company to get financing than through common shares or stocks.

Bull market: This is when a group of stocks or securities are expected to rise. If someone says they are "bullish about a stock," it means they expect it to rise. Or someone may say they are bullish about the market, which means they anticipate the market is rising or the price of stocks is rising.

Compound interest: Compound interest is interest added to the principal of a deposit or loan so that the added interest also earns interest from then on. For example, a bank account with $1000 initial principal and 20% interest per year would have a balance of $1200 at the end of the first year, $1440 at the end of the second year, $1728 at the end of the third year, and so on.

Common shares: These shares are available for purchase on a stock exchange and represent a portion of a company that the company has sold off to investors.

Cost of living: The cost of goods and services. Often referred to as "inflation." Usually given as a measure, for example: inflation is at 2%, meaning the cost of goods and services is rising in price at a rate of 2%. (See "Inflation")

Difference between stocks and bonds: A stock is a share of a company, a type of security that represents ownership and a claim on part of the company's earnings and assets. There are two main types of stock: common and preferred. A common stock usually entitles the owner to vote at shareholders' meetings and to receive dividends. Preferred stocks generally do not have voting rights but have a higher claim on assets and earnings than common shares. Owners of preferred stocks receive dividends before common shareholders and have priority in the event that a company goes bankrupt and is liquidated.

Dollar cost averaging: Dollar cost averaging (DCA) is an investment strategy in which someone invests in equal amounts of a stock on a regular basis over a period of time. For example, someone might invest $100 a month for five years to purchase shares of Rogers Communications. When they do this, the share value will change at different times, averaging the dollar cost of the shares.

Diversification: This is a term used to describe the process of spreading out investments over different investment categories.

For example, someone could diversify their portfolio between different bonds and stocks, or between different industries: oil and gas, banking, forestry, mining, etc. The benefits to diversifying an investment are that it potentially reduces risk by creating a balance between highs and lows.

Fees and commissions: It doesn't matter who we work with or what type of investments we buy, we will be charged fees. Ask what the fees are for any particular investment.

Exchange Traded Funds (ETF): ETFs track performance of a basket of stocks and trade throughout the day on the stock exchange. You can buy and sell these in the open markets. Mutual funds hold stocks and values are set at the end of each trading day.

Inflation: Inflation refers to the process through which the growing price of goods and services rises and falls over time. As prices rise, money purchases less. As prices fall (which is not often) money purchases more. Inflation impacts what is called "purchasing power," which is how much we can get with $1.00. Countries use a term called CPI, Consumer Price Index, to measure changes over time. Inflation can erode our ability to afford things. If inflation is rising at 2% and someone is only earning 1% in their savings account, their money is not keeping up with inflation. And this example does not even factor in taxes. On the other hand, money invested in a common share that is growing and earning 8% per year with inflation at 2%, allows someone to be further ahead in their ability to purchase things.

Rate of return: A profit on an investment over a period of time, expressed as a proportion of the original investment. The time period is typically a year, in which case the rate of return is referred to as *annual return*. Risk measures the chance of investment loss. Higher risk = higher potential loss; lower risk = lower rate of return.

Time value of money: How our money grows over time. Money invested today will grow bigger for tomorrow. For example, money put into a savings account today will grow into a much bigger balance over time. This assumes that money put in a savings account will earn interest and this interest, when compounded over time, will help money grow bigger.

Liquidity: This refers to how easily an investment can be turned into cash should it be needed. A money market fund, for example, can easily be turned into cash.

Mutual funds and exchange traded funds: Many new investors will invest money in mutual funds, otherwise known as exchange traded funds. They are simply a basket of stocks. They trade on the stock exchange, like stocks, and they can hold other investments, such as bonds and commodities.

Mutual funds: Many new investors will invest money in mutual funds. They are simply a basket of stocks. They trade on the stock exchange, like stocks, and they can hold other investments, such as bonds and commodities. There are fees associated with mutual funds and these vary.

Time value of money: The time value of money takes into account numerous factors: interest paid on money, inflation and taxes and rates of return on money. For example, $1.00 today will be worth more if invested. If it isn't, inflation or cost of living will erode its value and you will have less money to spend.

Risk tolerance: This term refers to the level of risk involved in investing. Generally speaking, higher risk investments tend to have the potential to generate higher rates of return, where lower risk investments tend to have the potential to generate lower rates of return.

Stock exchanges: A stock exchange is a place where buyers and sellers meet to exchange, purchase and sell stocks, bonds, and other investments. The New York Stock Exchange is the largest in the world, based on market capitalization and the number of trades conducted. In the old days, many brokers would meet in person to buy and sell shares of a company. Today, most trades are done electronically.

Major stock exchanges in North America include The New York Stock Exchange, The TSX or Toronto Stock Exchange, and NASDAQ. Around the world, the major stock exchanges are the Tokyo Stock Exchange, London Stock Exchange, and Hong Kong Stock Exchange.

The Best Chefs in the World

Allen, Colin. "The Benefits of Meditation." Psychology Today. Last modified June 6, 2012. http://www.psychologytoday.com

American Savings Education Council. Employee Benefit Research Institute. Accessed March 2013. http://www.ebri.org

Anthony, Mitch. *Life Transitions Top Ten Report.* Mitch Anthony's Institute for Financial Life Planning, 2007.

BMO Bank of Montreal. "BMO Bank of Montreal Psychology of Spending Report: Impulse Shopping a Costly Habit for Canadians." Market wire. Last modified September 25, 2012. http://newsroom.bmo.com

Buffett, Warren. *The Snowball: Warren Buffett and the Business of Life.* New York: Bantam, 2008.

Buffett, Warren. "Warren Buffett is bullish . . . on women." CNN Money. Last modified May 2, 2013. Accessed June 2013. http://money.cnn.com

Burns Kingsbury, Kathleen. "How to Give Financial Advice to Couples." KBK Wealth Connection: Creating Wealth From The Inside Out. Last modified 2013. http://www.kbkwealthconnection.com

Canadian Women's Foundation. "Fact Sheet: Moving Women Out of Poverty." http://www.canadianwomen.org/sites

CBC News, The National. The State of Canada, 11/12/14.

Chernoff, Sandy. *5 Secrets to Effective Communication.* Promontory Press, 2013.

Chu, Linda. Out of Chaos: Professional Organizing Solutions. Personal Interview August 2013. http://www.outofchaos.ca

Clements, Jonathan. "Putting a Price Tag on Life's Financial Goals." *Citi Bank Blog.* December 17, 2012. http://blog.citigroup.com

Consumer Reports. Accessed January 2013. http://www.consumerreports.org

Covey, Steven R. *The 7 Habits of Highly Effective People.* New York: Free Press, 1989.

Cox, Kathleen. "We all want to be housewives now." The Age: Life & Style. Last modified January 10, 2011. Accessed April 2013. http://www.theage.com.au

Daily Mail (www.dailymail.co.uk) Article on Love Really Is. Happy Relationships Help Many of us Thrive.

Deaton, Kahneman, Farrer, Straus, and Giroux. "High Income Improves Evaluation of Life But Not Emotional Well-being." *Psychological and Cognitive Sciences* 107, no. 38 (2010): 16489-16493.

Dunn, Elizabeth and Norton, Michael. *Happy Money: The Science of Smarter Spending.* New York: Simon & Schuster, 2013.

Duxbury, Linda and Higgins, Christopher. "Carleton Releases 2012 National Study on Balancing Work and Care giving in Canada." Carleton

Newsroom. Last modified October 25, 2012. Accessed March 2013. http://newsroom.carleton.ca

Erickson, Beth. "5 Ways Sharing Finances Can Be Bad for Your Marriage." *US News and World Report.* http://money.usnews.com

Feeney, Brook, Dr. Carnegie Mellon University in Pittsburgh and Professor Nancy Collins, of the University of California at Santa Barbara.

FINRA Investor Education Foundation. "Take the Financial Literacy Quiz." National Financial Capability Study. Last modified 2013. http://www.usfinancialcapability.org/quiz.php

Financial Planning Standards Council, http://www.fpsc.ca. Get More Out of Life.

Freedman, David H. "Time-Warping Temptations." *Scientific American Mind* 24, no. 1 (2013): 45-49.

Gallup-Healthways. Well-Being Index. http://www.well-beingindex.com

Hildred, Stafford and Ewbank, Tim. *Jamie, King of the Kitchen. The Biography of the Man Who Revolutionised the Way Britain Eats.* John Blake Publishing, 2012.

Huffington Post. "Hillary Clinton On What Designers She Wears: 'Would You Ever Ask A Man That Question?'" Huff Post Style. Last modified May 25, 2011. http://www.huffingtonpost.com

Huffington Post. "Gender Wage Gap", 2013/09/17.

Intuit Canada. http://www.intuit.com. Simplify The Business of Life. Accessed May 2013.

Maslow, Abraham. *Motivation and Personality.* New York: Harper & Row, 1954.

Media Release: "Australian pocket money economy sits at $1.4 billion per annum." Commonwealth Bank of Australia. Last modified February 4, 2013. Accessed February 2013. https://www.commbank.com.au

Merrill Lynch 2013 Survey in Satran, Richard. "5 Ways Sharing Finances Can Be Bad for Your Marriage." *US News and World Report.* http://money.usnews.com/money/personal-finance/mutual-funds

Milevsky, Moshe A. and Macqueen, Alexandra. *Pensionize Your Nest Egg: How to Use Product Allocation to Create a Guaranteed Income for Life.* Mississauga, Wiley & Sons Canada, Ltd: 2010.

Powel, Julie. *Julie & Julia, 365 days, 524 recipes, 1 tiny apartment kitchen.* Little, Brown and Company, Time Warner Group, September 2005.

Pudrovska and Amelia Karraker. "Gender, Job Authority, and Depression," published in the December issue of the *Journal of Health and Social Behavior.*

Scott, Rick, Cryder, Cynthia, and Loewenstein, George. "Tightwads and Spendthrifts." *Journal of Consumer Research* 34, no. 6 (2008): 767-782.

Silva, Mark. "Michelle Obama: '120-percenter' Blog." Chicago Tribune: Mayflower Voyage. Last modified May 7, 2009. http://www.chicagotribune.com/topic/arts-culture/history

Silverstein, Michael J. and Sayre, Kate. *Women Want More*. New York: HarperCollins, 2009.

Soman, Dilip and Mazar, Nina. "Financial literacy is not enough." *The Hill Times* 24, no 1165 (2012): 25. www.hilltimes.com

Stanley, Thomas and Danko, William. *The Millionaire Next Door*, Taylor Trade Publishing, 1996, 2010.

State Street Bank. SPDR University. Last modified 2013. http://www.spdru.com

Statistic Canada. www.statscan.ca: *Average household food expenditure, by province (Canada)*.

Stevenson, Betsey and Wolfers, Justin. "Subjective Well-Being and Income: Is There Any Evidence of Satiation?" *American Economic Review*. Last modified April 16, 2013. http://www.brookings.edu

The Certified Coaches Federation (CCF), www.certifiedcoachesfederatio.com. Course Syllabus, Fenelon Falls, Ontario, Canada.

The Investment Funds Institute of Canada (IFIC), www.ific.ca. Informed Investor Supplement. The Value of Financial Advice. Produced by The Investment Funds Institute of Canada in conjunction with the Custom Content Group of The Globe and Mail.

The Richard Ivey School of Business, Executive MBA, Course syllabus. Glenn Rowe. Corporate Strategy.

The US Census Bureau, (www.census.gov). Data on Aging of the American Population.

Tuttle, Brad. "A Mom's Work Is Worth $113K Annually. Or Maybe About Half That." Time: Business & Money. Last modified April 30, 2012. Accessed March 2013.

Not Your Average Home Cooks

To learn more about the art of cooking, please visit www.juliachild.com or www.jaimeoliver.com.

Healthy Aging for Women (www.healthyagingforwomen.com). Learn about how to be vibrant, healthy and strong as you age.

How to live to 100.com (www.bluezones.com). Dan Buettner and his team study the world's "Blue Zones," communities whose elders live to record-setting ages.

The Financial Planning Standard Council (www.fpsc.ca). To find a certified financial planner or to learn more about the benefits of financial planning.

Rob Carrick (www.robcarrick.com). Personal finance and wealth management advice. His advice is practical and straightforward.

Statistics Canada (www.statcan.gc.ca). Information on women's health and aging.

Dr. Milevsky (www.yorku.ca/milevsky). Dr. Milvesky is a professor at York University. He is well respected in the industry and offers practical advice on retirement. His book *Pensionize Your Nest Egg: How to Use Product Allocation to Create a Guaranteed Income for Life* includes everything you need to know to create your own pension plan in retirement.

www.ingramcontent.com/pod-product-compliance
Lightning Source LLC
Chambersburg PA
CBHW040552010526
44110CB00054B/2642